THE FALL OF
WESTERN
CIVILIZATION

Published by Entropy Works LLP, India
www.TheFallofWesternCivilization.com

Printed by CreateSpace
Charleston, SC, 29406
USA

ISBN 978-93-5300-670-9

THE FALL OF WESTERN CIVILIZATION

How Liberalism is
Destroying the West from Within

SHIVAJI LOKAM

Contents

Preface	1
Introduction	3
1. The Origins and the Nature of Liberalism	9
2. Nomenclature, Timelines, and Concepts	31
3. Understanding the Nomenclature	51
4. Fallout from Nineteenth Century Liberalism	71
5. Liberalism Unfolding in Twentieth Century	93
6. Critical Analysis of Classical Liberalism	127
7. Critical Analysis of Modern Liberalism	145
8. Republicanism to Liberalism in the United States	171
9. The Rescuing of the West	181
10. The Errors of Enlightenment – Part One	191
11. The Errors of Enlightenment – Part Two	201
12. The Ultimate Causes of the 2008 Financial Crisis	217
13. Liberalism and the Future	241
Conclusion	259
Data Sources	261
Bibliography	263
Index	273

Preface

The book as initially planned would have covered the story of unraveling only along the economic dimension of the wealthy western nations – that being an account of original economic analysis, economic history including the causes of the Great Depression and the 2008 Financial Crisis, and the future going forward. But having realized that the understanding of the majestic events of the twentieth century and its bearings in our present times remains poor, the social and political dimension naturally called out. Even as the causes of many of those events like the First World War were firmly rooted within the economic dimension, the consequences nevertheless had projected onto the socio-political dimension. Therefore it became inevitable that a complete snapshot and analysis of the recent economic history of Western civilization has to have all of the critical dimensions of civilization. It was from that task that the notion of the Western civilization seemingly in a state of decline had come to the fore. And that became the overarching theme knitting the larger story at work, hence this book's title!

Introduction

This book aims to fill the longstanding, latent gap in the literature that had become inadequate in many ways to understand the glorious transformative trends underpinning life and politics across the Western civilization today. To meaningfully grasp the present and capture a snapshot of the future, this book grippingly recaptures the last two-hundred-and-fifty years history. When told captivatingly and correctly, history aids quite well in the efforts to project a possible and convincing trajectory of the condition of life on earth going forward.

Notably, we'll navigate through the rise and decline, understand the ebb and flow of the critical and variant forces of industry, technology, polity, and institutions stretching back in time as much as possible. We'll see how the interplay of those forces split into series of phases over time had influenced the flow of history. And we'll also see how the unceasingly influential eighteenth and nineteenth century Liberalism invariably played into causing or precipitating such majestic events as the French Revolution, the First World War, the rise of Socialism, Communism, Fascism, Progressivism, the Second World War, Cold War, and Decolonization.

Also, we'll see how those historical forces, operating under wholly different phases, and congruent with the twentieth century Liberalism, have influenced the postwar events, such as Cultural Revolution, Financial Crisis, and Western societal decline and decay. We'll also see how those forces will continue to have a major impact going into the future. It, therefore, follows that a critical study of the doctrine of Liberalism is central to the task at hand.

Many prominent writers fall into the ideological trap of this philosophical and political doctrine that is Liberalism and about which we are duly concerned as a matter of great deal and subject throughout the book. Ordinarily, the tales of history drip with this potent ideology from end to end, unwittingly contaminating the narrative in the process. Parroting a mainstream thinking, the writers, thereby, often leave the reader with twisted events to reckon with and blindsided from reality.

As an example, the title of this book may not entirely comport with the narrative held dearly by historians and political pundits. Even if it may, the idea of Western civilization in a state of decline for them is something to be reckoned with and looked forward to seeing it unfold in practice if not actively contributing to it.

Many unwittingly are trying to understand a game that they play an active part of and usually are blind to the caricatures of their making. Liberal historians and pundits writing about history and present-day politics that is very much shaped and influenced by the doctrine of Liberalism may be akin to the trap we encounter as the mind tries to understand itself. This tumultuous crisis of trapped narrative even in regards to how we perceive current events is something I tried to wholly escape from in this book.

Besides the inadequacy of the literature, failures to grasp the current state of affairs in another way and to a certain degree is because of the abysmal state of the discipline of economics that for over two-hundred years now has consistently and successfully remained as a home to theorizing pure fiction.

Given such a dismal state of the dismal science that is economics, all efforts to capture the full story end up futile. That has to be corrected. For one, it is impossible to imagine a case in which a critical study of a society and its polity may be complete, cut off from the synthetic analysis of that which is responsible for the melody of civilization: resolving the problem of mobilizing available resources. In other words, economic dimension to explaining historical events takes the central seat. For Western civilization has been in the midst of winding down of industrialization and modernization drive for some decades now, it is imperative we undertake original analysis to adequately and effectively contribute to the economic dimension of the story.

Herein lies the reason I had pressed myself to write this book and as such I believe it is for the same that this book may be of great value for the reader. Sensing the possibility of telling a wholesome story that fulfills the two dimensions – a recapture of events of history free from the trap of Liberalism and liberal narrative, and an account of original economic analysis and its implications to the story at the purpose – that this book had come to be conceived.

Especially in regards to the latter – the economic dimension – being the fruits of two years of research I undertook for the upcoming book *The General Theory of Rapid Economic Development*, that I bring an original account to a vast degree. With that advantage, I take a new shot at exploring the underlying economic impulses to history and historical events, especially of the recent past, in conjunction with an examination of the discipline of economics itself. In fact, a significant derivative of this exploratory work is of the success found in clinching the ultimate causes of the 2008 Financial Crisis that is reported for the first time in this book.

Besides that portion of novelty along the economic dimension, the account of the nineteenth century economic shocks and the role those had played in precipitating major disasters of the early twentieth century is not new at all. Economic historian Karl Polanyi laid it all out in his book *The*

Great Transformation (1944). But even that episode, surprisingly, is misunderstood or misinterpreted. For example, the revolutionary insurgents and political writers back then, such as Lenin, seemingly assumed that Capitalism and Imperialism were thoroughly intertwined. Believing the same, leaders of nations that became independent after the Second World War resented the former and moved away from it to avoid the links it had with the latter. The backdrop for such conclusion rested on the gross misunderstanding of the kind of economic system the West had during the nineteenth century. That part remains unclear for many to this day.

Finally, the observation that the West is in a state of steady decline is also not new. It has been told and retold numerous times and multiple places that still remain partly obscure; even as this book's title is merely a different version encapsulating essentially the same meaning in titles as old as *Suicide of the West*, or as recent as *The Strange Death of Europe*.

Notwithstanding the same, I take particular interest throughout the book in the identification and the direction of causation of events. And importantly, I thread everything together and tell one complete story. There is anyway the old recurring problem of the difficulty in the identification of causation in history, but we shall come back to this issue in Chapter One.

Lastly, I believe this book can serve, without overwhelming with information, of which I tried to keep it minimal, to critically engage the mind of the reader, and to contribute to the development of a degree of skepticism of the received things. And in fact, that may be the enduring value imparted from the book.

Chapter One

The Origins and the Nature of Liberalism

Western Civilization at the Turn

Hundred years ago today in Russia the Bolsheviks stormed the Winter Palace, led a coup d'état against the Provisional Government, fought and won the Civil war and then went on to rule for the next seventy years. In that year of 1917, while the European powers were still fighting out the Great War, the Russian revolutionaries had unmistakably determined that they would chart the course of the country on their revolutionary terms, on their peculiar mental constructs, on their distinctive criterion of merits and demerits. Such was the course divergence that it was wholly radical and polar opposite to what all of Western civilization had come to be at that point since when that way of life may be traced to its emergence or reemergence sometime in 700 AD in the middle of European continent.

Something had gone wrong. The Russian Empire seemed to be adequately on the path toward embracing what Western Europe and the US had accomplished up to that point. It began modest industrialization drive, initiated political reforms after losing the War against Japan in 1905 – two significant developments in the realms of economy and polity that surely meant further ripple effects down the line. However Russia had soon found itself in a quagmire. The Entente powers of Europe including Russia divided into two factions went to War that for about four years had seemed to go nowhere. In the middle of 1915, Russia was fighting a war of attrition. The inept Russian Monarch Nicholas II took over the Supreme Command and went to the battlefront leaving Empress Alexandra in charge of the affairs of the state. Having stacked the Court with corrupt and incompetent ministers, the Empress became the real autocrat in the Russian capital. The governance suffered, and the civilian population dreaded the inadequate supplies. Soon the public had come to see the war as a lost cause not least of all because of the suspicion that the Empress with her German origins and relations was an active German spy at the Court. The rising influence of the Empress and her "holy friend' Rasputin caused political tension between the public and the government. The claims that the two were working for the Germans and that they had a direct line to Berlin were circulated and believed. The angry public was inflamed by the rumors of treason. The conditions of utter discontent ushered in the revolutionary mood to revolt against the monarchy. Soon the chain of events from there led to the overthrow of the Russian Tsar by the public and then of the temporary government that followed the Monarch rule by the Bolsheviks.

That climax was a moment of reckoning for Western civilization because that development had led to not only further losses to the West after a few decades but also had morphed into a significant threat to the West during the Cold War. As per the Marxist theory, socialism should never have occurred first in the semi-agrarian, rural Russia; the country has had to first pass through the capitalist stage of history. Socialism follows the so-called 'bourgeois-democratic revolution' and does not precede it. For that reason, even Lenin at first seemed hesitant to stage a coup. Those were mystifying times.

With the benefit of hindsight, one who is looking far and wide could see that in those given circumstances the Russian detour, temporary or permanent, actually represented a larger and significant crisis escalating for some time in Western Europe, that the Russian detour was more of an accidental epiphenomena– sort of a byproduct of an actual mega-development.

The crisis plaguing Western Europe at the turn of the twentieth century lay in the tumultuous transformation of life, work and politics that were shaken to the core partly by ongoing industrialization, international trade and colonization, and all of the institutions erected or conceived to support them. The welcomed responses to that crisis in each country, just as in the case of Russia, came from the intellectual heartlands crisscrossing the continent with Switzerland acting as the unofficial headquarters. The times were such that the revolutionary mood everywhere guaranteed those same but flavored responses that swept in short time after the Russian Revolution, the Italian peninsula, the German heartland, the Iberian peninsula and flirted too well with the British island.

The unexpected developments in the European continent at that time were a single response to the accumulated failures resulting from a philosophical and a political doctrine that was Liberalism – or more specifically, that what is known today as Classical Liberalism. The assumed response to tackle the shortcomings directly came in different forms at different places, fully acclimatized to and emerging from the national conditions of the time, and had at the core a dialectical feature known as Collectivism – one such derivative of it being Modern Liberalism.

This book is simply an account and an analysis of events of history but with a special focus on how Classical Liberalism before the crisis and Modern Liberalism as a response to tackling it played the dominant role. This is a book telling the story of what had led to the failures of Classical Liberalism and how that had played into causing the monumental events of the first half of the twentieth century. It also tells the story of how the assumed response in the form of Modern Liberalism had failed the West again and how that has ever since been playing into causing the crises of our present times.

It conclusively follows that we need to dig into this familiar but strange at times, omnipresent but obscure to many, influential but impotent in the hinterland, doctrine of Liberalism – its meaning, its intellectual forbearers, its mystical self-sustaining transformation, its mental capacity and weight, and importantly its relationship with reality.

Liberalism – It's Meaning and History

The intellectual weight tagging the term 'Liberalism' comes from its Latin root "liber" meaning "free" – and therefore it's always a question of freedom from whom that this doctrine known as Liberalism represents. Originally the term connoted philosophy of freedom but strictly referred to the freedom of the individual.

Like all doctrines, Liberalism is a body of thought developed over time, and only in the post-development phase that Liberalism took the name thus. The task of painting a neat history of Liberalism is methodically challenging for one of many reasons that the subject is crude, not suitably organized, and can claim to its lineage multiple bodies of thought as varied as sixteenth and seventeenth-century Rationalism to mid-eighteenth century Social Contract theory of Frenchmen Rousseau to early nineteenth century Positivism. Moreover, the doctrine was transformed in the metamorphosis of thought along one dimension at least, adapting with historical forces. Despite so, we may try to understand it more clearly by identifying its beliefs and axioms in the few critical dimensions of life.

Liberalism's distinct origins lay in the seventeenth and eighteenth century rationalism, and to that effect, the earliest intellectual forbearers of this doctrine can be traced to Francis Bacon (1561 – 1626) and Rene Descartes (1596 – 1650).

Rationalism was a movement that held the belief that reason alone should be the basis for the establishment of truth. That as a matter of historical consistency stands as the core axiom underpinning Liberalism; and at any time there arise specific misconceptions concerning the doctrine, one may safely seek full refugee at that axiom and frame the matter at hand through that lens. The premise that reason should stand at the center of everything found its prominent historical artifact in the French Revolution when the revolutionaries renamed the Notre Dame Cathedral the "Temple of Reason," with the words "To Philosophy" carved into the façade of the Gothic cathedral. Those were the revolutionary times that the "Cult of Reason" was the established state religion.

The next stopping point from there is the doctrine's belief about the nature of man, and here again, it falls back on the conception of "reason." On that critical note that so much underpins the full stock of Liberalism's beliefs, values, and ideals, the role of reason had not been so much about logically deducing. It instead functioned to reason that the virtue of "reason" is the missing link in the transformation of the presently unfavorable nature of Man to the one of favorable. Liberalism supposes that a cruel society exists because of the lack of reason taking a central place to reign in the affairs of individual and society. The journey from the evil and wicked society to the good society is only a matter of adopting reason in all places. That thinking naturally extends to mean that man is infallible if not for his ignorance (and this has many other implications, as we'll see later on) that is the ultimate source of evil and the reason for faulty society still reigning in. Therefore Liberalism firmly believes that human nature is plastic, that the nature of Man is not fixed but changing, with an indefinite potential for favorable development.

Again, Bacon and Descartes can be credited here; they were the ones in the modern times who had launched the first assault on the traditional view of human nature that regarded that Man is fallible, partly corrupt, had a permanent, unchanging property. We'll come back to discussing more this contrasting viewpoint in the context of instituting a lawful government. For now, the recognition of the divergent view Liberalism took on human nature suffices. Anyway, it was the Age of Bacon that precipitated into an early wave of thinking that placed reason and experiment at the highest level of virtue, giving full thrust to the Scientific revolution that followed it.

Having affirmed that reason stands at the high altar, we may now begin to understand Liberalism in a more dimensional form. The many dimensions of life and society come down to political, economic, religious and tradition. In the political dimension, Liberalism is firmly opposed to specific abuses, which have to be eliminated at any rate. Above all, it opposes absolute monarchy and the old-style, tyrannical state. Second, it rigidly opposes the old-style stratification of the social order, that being the privileged positions of the clergy and the nobility. Third, Liberalism is against the tie between church and state – the "anticlerical attitude." Fourth, it advocates a democratic form of government and universal suffrage – the "one man, one vote" right as part of the democratic system. This fourth front essentially being the pillar on which the opposition to the first and second was constructed.

In the economic dimension, Liberalism opposes the old legal restrictions that set limits to free economic activity. The enlightened (rational) self-interested individual should be the only motive behind conducting economic activity. Further, the doctrine held that the concerted actions of self-interested individuals lead to stable, harmonious order in society.

On the religion dimension, Liberalism is anti-religious. Whereas the anticlerical attitude of the separation of church and state comes down to the political front, the doctrine goes much further here. Liberalism thoroughly rejects revelation and dogma as the source of truth; it scraps religious substance and turns secular and ideological. That view can be ascertained to its assumption of the autonomy of inherent human reason as the source of all knowledge and truth – essentially a counterpart to its scientific front that seeks freedom from "authority" not only from dogmatism but also from classical philosophy. Discarding spiritual substance, Liberalism is wholly secular. But the doctrine in practice goes beyond that. It strives to eradicate all religious influence to absolutely usher in a secular world that operates based on reason alone.

Lastly, on the tradition dimension, Liberalism besides rejecting faith opposes custom, intuition, authority, prejudice, superstition, sentiment and habits. As is only consistent for a doctrine that holds reason as the basis for the establishment of all truth, the ideas, conceptions, and practices descendant of the irrational past must be curtailed for "reason" to prevail above all else.

Having outlined the various dimensional fronts of Liberalism and with its view on the nature of man clear, it is useful now to state that Liberalism in practice exhibits certain tendencies, inclinations commonly displayed among its faithful. With "reason" taking the central place, Liberalism believes all bad societies can and should be transformed into good societies – that is, free human beings would order the society rationally with autonomous reason. That in practice comes down to education that therefore acts as the primary vehicle – and a good starting point – to achieving that society. In conjunction with its belief and advocacy for universal suffrage and democracy, free, educated men through their vote discard the bad institutions and enact the good institutions to chart the society to greater glory. Therefore, the stress on education and democracy for enlightened, rational men using reason to achieve the good society means Liberalism believes in and advocates freedom of speech. The intellectual forebear of free speech in the modern times may be traced to its most famous defender, Voltaire (1694 – 1778) who also advocated for religious tolerance, the separation of church and state, and reason in the affairs of the individual.

Because Liberalism believes the source of bad society ultimately hinges on the ignorance of man – and not having to do with any innate characteristics of him, the roadblock to achieving the good society, therefore, is external (to man), which can be remedied by universal education programs. That is educated enlightened individual acting according to autonomous reason participate in democracy and by using his right to free speech and one vote under the principle of equal universal suffrage enact the good institutions that can then transform the evil society to good society. The belief in the tendencies toward the good society that is just around the corner is the source of historical optimism expressed by Liberalism.

Liberalism – It's Development, Influence and Reach

It was in the first two dimensions – political and economic – that Liberalism made great strides in theory and practice by mid-nineteenth century across the West. On the other two fronts, it had to wait until it was allowed the full reign due to specific historical developments that in practice essentially followed after the first two fronts had become fulfilled.

It should be noted that like every other doctrine Liberalism incorporated into its body those ideas congruent with the times and conjunction with other historical developments. Like an opportunist, the doctrine milks watershed events to its potential to advance its ideals and beliefs. That is, even if the ideas of the doctrine were fully developed it may in practice become wholly contingent upon the circumstantial events of history to get implemented. For example, it was only after the advent of Darwinian science of human origins that the doctrine saw full thrust to the realization of its ideal of anti-religious attitude within the society. However, even before this development Liberalism displayed those tendencies in practice. The fitting example of this is the French revolution that satisfied the thirst of the revolutionary mob to implement the ideas of anti-religious views long before the advent of Darwinian science.

To the religious and tradition front, the full intellectual thrust came from Darwin's tome, and also from Nietzsche's attacks on traditional morality, instigating and stimulating the Great Awakening and about which we'll learn more. Having incorporated necessary changes to its economic front – which saw it going from rational individualism to state intervention of economy, Liberalism in the twentieth century emerged with a full new thrust to achieve in practice its ideals on the religious and tradition front as well.

Therefore along the political and economic dimensions that Liberalism with the advocacy for the values of "freedom" and "liberty" from late eighteenth century to late nineteenth century had come to see those ideals turn into reality. And to this political and economic dimension-focused version of Liberalism we have come to call it *Classical Liberalism*. Along the religious and traditional front, and the modified economic front, that Liberalism with the advocacy for the values of "equality" and "justice" from early twentieth century to early twenty-first century had come to see the ideals turn into reality. And to this social and economic dimension-focused version of Liberalism we have come to call it *Modern Liberalism*.

On the political dimension, the pillars upon which Liberalism constructed opposition to absolute monarchy and tyrannical government were demands for basic human rights and universal suffrage. Liberalism strongly opposes the suffrage principle based on property and, or education, as it manifestly believes in "one man, one vote" principle only.

Political theorist John Locke (1632 – 1704) laid the foundations of political dimension of Liberalism most famously in his two-part work *Two Treatises of Government* (1690), in which he attacked the divine rights of the king and argued that the individual has a natural right to life, liberty, and property.

Locke refuted the traditional concept of the divine right of the King to rule, rationalizing that only when human beings moved out of their natural state of wilderness to unite into a civilian group that came to occupy a fixed territory constituted in effect a political society. That was the basis, Locke wrote and championed, for the institution of a lawful government; the consent of the governed reigned supreme over any such supernatural rights to rule. Locke also advocated in his work for religious tolerance.

Locke's conception of civil society influenced the theorists of the Age of Enlightenment, but in the matters of government tyranny, they went beyond Locke's envisioned socio-political order. The political theorists proclaimed that the purpose of the government was to protect individuals from being harmed by others, but they also fretted on the thought that the government itself can pose a threat to individual freedom. The coercive power of the state is at best "a necessary evil," as Thomas Paine (1737 – 1809) observed in *Common Sense* (1776).

In short, Liberalism on the political front believed in and advocated for the liberal state.

On the economic dimension, Liberalism advocated the laissez-faire (let it be free) attitude on the part of the state in the matters of the economy. It was believed that the rational self-interested individual operating under market forces serves the greater good of the society. David Hume (1711 – 1776), Adam Smith (1723 – 1790) and David Ricardo (1772 – 1823) together laid the foundations of classical economic theory. With the publication of the Scottish Philosopher Adam Smith's magnum opus *The Wealth of Nations* (1776), the idea of liberalization of economy from the grips of state captured the imagination. Hume's *Political Discourses* (1752), Smith's *Wealth of Nations* and Ricardo's *On the Principles of Political Economy and Taxation* (1817) were the requisite buildings blocks of the ideas shaped into the monetary system of Gold standard, the Self-regulating market, and free trade.

In short, Liberalism on the economic front believed in and advocated for the laissez-faire economy. This position reversed at the turn of the twentieth century and about which we'll learn more later on.

In both arenas, political and economic – that is, the liberalization of the state to creating the liberal state, and to formulating the laissez-faire economy – it was Great Britain that not only laid the intellectual foundations but also led in practice, inspiring many countries to follow its lead. On political theory, John Locke led, and Jean-Jacques Rousseau (1712 – 1778) followed, as both in their right became prominent because of the roles they played in the revolutionary spirit engulfed on both sides of the English Channel lapsed by a century. The Glorious Revolution (1688) – often called the Bloodless Revolution – deposed the King and permanently forbid him from exercising absolute rule. The chartering of the Bill of Rights (1689) and the establishment of the supremacy of the British Parliament can be understood to be the first victory in the fight for individual freedom.

It was to support and reinforce the grand achievement and give it the intellectual basis that John Locke penned the two treatises, the first of which is merely a point-by-point refutation of Robert Filmer's *Patriarcha* (1680) that argued for absolute hereditary monarchy by the Scripture. In his second treatise, Locke underscored many thematic points related to representative government, the right of the people to revolt, the protection of property and liberty. About a century later across the English Channel, these ideas further developed by Frenchman Jean-Jacques Rousseau had carried into the revolutionary document approved at the National Assembly during the French Revolution (1789 – 1794). Rousseau in the mode of the revolutionary thinking characteristic of the time had ushered in a political thought that may be hard to pin down the entirety of it as the lineage from Locke, but inspired and shaped the political dimension of the doctrine of Liberalism in theory and in practice. We'll revisit the French Revolution in more detail later on.

Revolutions inspired by the political ideals of Liberalism have been the primary mechanism by which the liberal transformation of the state had been carried out. The Declaration of Independence and the Revolutionary War, the French Revolution, the Glorious Revolution all belongs to this category. Also falling under the same radar are the freedom movements across the Global South and the East as the same ideals later on inspired and energized the spirited leaders advocating for self-government to mount revolutionary struggles and movements for independence.

On the economic arena, Liberalism opposed state involvement in the free movement of labor nationally. Thus establishing the first competitive labor market in England in 1834 with the passage of the Poor Law Amendment– essential to the operations of market economy. Before this development, labor was prevented from forming a national market by having in place strict restrictions on its physical mobility, having him consigned to the countryside Parish. Land and money mobilized in England before labor was; thus the creation of the national labor market in 1834 by abolishing the "right to live" provisions in a 1795 law that was designed to provide relief to the poor can be considered as the starting point of nineteenth century Capitalism.

Liberalism & Republicanism

It is almost unquestionably observed today that the American founding fathers were a product of Enlightenment indeed inspired by Locke's vision of natural rights of man and that, therefore, Liberalism – the shining beacon of thought developed during the Age of Enlightenment – also underpins the American project. That to put it plainly does not capture the full essence of the distinct world outlook the founders shared. The premise that which ultimately inspired them to envision and create a bold future for America may be referenced as "Republicanism" to aid in amplifying that distinction.

The Age of Enlightenment was a fertile environment in which men had debated complex ideas, taking inspiration from the progress of fellow theorists but had strong convictions of their own. The Age spawned various strands of political doctrines that interject partly, but differ widely. Liberalism and Republicanism are two such philosophies sharing certain ideals such as freedom of speech, but grossly divergent in the underlying thesis such as the views on human nature. That is, on a superficial level, the ideals shared between them do not necessarily appear to present a stark divergence, but do have a profound distinction in the philosophy, as a matter of fact, which we'll reflect upon shortly.

The American founding fathers although they were a product of European Enlightenment rejected Liberalism's view on human nature because they did not believe human nature, at its core, as the liberal doctrine holds, is plastic. Instead, they tightly held the belief that human nature is unchanging, and by all means, it is not perfect, and even after the intervention of state, it can never be. They did not repudiate the revelation and dogma. They strongly adhered to the belief that man has darker motives.

To check the incorrigibly corrupt side of man the founders envisaged a republican form of government and the checks and balances that come with it. They designed a system that through the constitutional mechanisms checks the everlasting thirst for power by men and to prevent the government from becoming tyrannical and oppressive – that is, they believed in limited government. Let's now see on what fronts the ideals of Liberalism and Republicanism differ and diverge.

On the political front, the founders envisaged a liberal state, but they went beyond that – beyond what the British Parliament been able to achieve. Influenced by Charles Montesquieu's (1689 – 1755) *The Spirit of the Laws* (1750) the founders firmly believed in the doctrine of Separation of Powers with inbuilt mechanisms to check the powers of each branch by others. Therefore a system of government with clearly defined and balanced separation of powers among the different branches remained a top priority for them. Keeping the branches of government separate to prevent the abuse of power paved the way in practice to a system of government gridlock with the Checks and Balances in place. Liberalism, as a matter of history, believes in one supreme body wielding the authority of the state to carry out the will of the people as expressed by their exercising the "one man, one vote" right as part of the democratic system.

Secondly, which goes back to this very aspect we just touched on, the founders rejected the textbook style democracy, as they thought this form of government would merely result in the rule by an elected mob. Instead, they created an Electoral College and instituted two senate-seats for every state (small and large) that Liberalism's concept of "one man, one vote" so diametrically collides. Besides, the Electoral College and the two Senate-seat concepts worked well to alleviate the concerns of smaller states who feared the bigger states would steamroll them in the Upper chamber. The originally devised method of electing senators to the Upper chamber by the respective state legislatures, which was later amended, acted as a way of representation of the states directly, circumventing the "one man, one vote" principle again.

So far, the first divergence arrived in regards to the government framework and operation, the second in regards to the election of the head of the executive and the representatives to the Legislature. Now, the third one is in regards to the approved limits to the powers of the central (federal) government. The founders firmly believed in limited government – and they envisioned this by explicitly enumerating the powers of the Legislature in the Constitution and by amending it with the Bill of Rights that cannot be taken away by a majority of people. Specifically, as enumerated in the Tenth Amendment, the powers not expressly delegated to the federal government by the Constitution, (nor prohibited by it to the states) are reserved to the states respectively, or to the people. In other words, the founders believed in Federalism and enacted a robust federal form of government that so invariably contrasts with and contradicts Liberalism's one-body legislature that has no explicit barriers to powers vested to it. Loosely, Federalism is anathema to Liberalism.

Another critical divergence lay in the relationship between the church and the state. Whereas Liberalism completely rejects any tie between religion and state, the founding fathers merely prohibited Congress from making any law establishing a religion and intervening in the free exercise of it. Nowhere in the Constitution had they declared the separation of religion and state. They instead inserted a clause prohibiting Congress from picking and choosing a religion and from forcing the individual to believe in and practice one or another.

But above all else, the founders believed in the concept of the sovereign people that unmistakably clashes with and diverges from Liberalism's belief in the notion of popular sovereignty as expressed in the universal suffrage. That in regards to the question of the source of power and the residual limits to it if there exist any, the differences between the two political doctrines most starkly comes to light. We'll comeback to this topic.

On the economic front, the founders envisaged a state that is again limited in its powers to intervene. And to that effect, they had enumerated certain powers to the Congress to regulate commerce with foreign nations and among the several states. The latter is the interstate commerce clause that stands disputed in the extent and range of the delegation of power and as such quite a few laws passed under that authority rested on the fate of the US Supreme Court ruling. Additionally, such powers as to borrow money, to coin money, lay and collect taxes, to appropriate money from the Treasury – essentially a laissez-faire attitude but enumerated with ample authority and latitude to intervene in the matters of coining money, foreign trade, taxation and interstate business.

On the religious front and the tradition front, the founders were stringently pro-religion and pro-tradition, or to put it mildly, they were not anti-religion and anti-tradition in any sense of the meaning.

Along these four fronts as on many others delineating from it, and to the issue of the views held on the nature of man, the ideals of Republicanism as the founders believed in and envisioned distinctly differ and diverge from the doctrine of Liberalism. One may now clearly see that the four-dimensional distinctions between the two directly or indirectly come down to the divergent opinions on the nature of man. It was by keeping in mind not the imagined perfect man but the wicked, corrupt man that the American founders had designed the Constitution.

Liberalism & Reality

By now we have taken an adequate stock of the doctrine of Liberalism to inevitably arrive at the question of its relationship with and clash against reality. Classical Liberalism – the political and economic dimension-focused version of Liberalism with the advocacy for the values of "freedom" and "liberty" – from late eighteenth century to late nineteenth century had come to see the ideals turn into reality, ignoring the other two fronts. Thus, by the mid-nineteenth century the liberal state and the laissez-faire economy – the two bulwarks of political and economic dimension – had turned into reality in Great Britain and the US (in the local flavor). The religious and tradition front of the doctrine remained in the back dormant. Many other Western countries (Russia and its enclaves exempted) later followed the model – few not until all the way up to the mid-twentieth century. In all of them, monarchies were eliminated or weakened; power centralized in a federal or central bicameral legislature; certain fundamental rights were enumerated – (the 1949 Basic Law in Germany, 1978 Spanish Constitution);

representative democracy made to work; church and state separated.

Modern Liberalism – the religious and traditional front, and the modified, economic front-focused version of Liberalism with the advocacy for the values of "equality" and "justice" – from early twentieth century to early twenty-first century had come to see the ideals turn into reality, ignoring the political front. Thus by the mid-twentieth century, a sizable secular society had emerged, unseen since Christianity became the official religion of the West. This trend over time all the way until the first decade of the twenty-first century is severe in all Western countries, except for the US. Because morality and tradition are partially downstream from religion, the West had since then felt the corresponding repercussions on the tradition front. On the modified economic front – that being the intervention-oriented state – the results are not unambiguous at all. During this century, government budgets, business regulations, central government and international-trade bureaucracy have all grown to unprecedented levels.

Liberalism, created from a systematic inquiry into the organization of life and society by the "optimists," "rationalists," "pessimists," "utopians," belonging to that milieu in all of the time on earth when the human mind lit the brightest, has harbored grand ambitions. It's grip on the individual, culture and politics strengthened ever since it became a thing. Classical Liberalism liberalized the state to free the individual and the economic system from the tyranny of monarchy and the privileged. Modern Liberalism liberalized the society to free the individual from the tyranny of religion and tradition. It is to that effect that the doctrine of Liberalism manifestly influenced the flow of history, shaped the life and the organization of society on earth.

The appraisal of Liberalism, of the collective success or failure of its contribution to the development of the condition of life on earth in the long-term hinges on the kind of relationship the full stock of the doctrine, or even the core axioms of it, has with reality. One concerning axiom is the role of reason, and another critical one that supposedly derives from it is the view on human nature. What special relationship those axioms underpinning the doctrine have with reality? There it is, one clue right there: Liberalism is, after all, a set of beliefs that in the collective bearing became a doctrine, "a body of thought," and for those who believe in it an ideology that may or may not wholly or partly comport with the reality. That intrinsic relationship of the doctrine with the reality or truth had become the decisive factor in shaping history, the most recent times and about which we'll discuss from one end to another throughout the book.

But before we proceed further it may serve to state briefly here, in the light of having skirted around with investigative lens, that the doctrine – together with the full stock of ideals, axioms, and beliefs – is specious, flawed, and deceptive in theory, and contradictory, unfruitful or unfavorable, and even dangerous in practice. At this point, the purpose of the rest of the Chapters comes to understanding why this may be the case or is the case – whichever the side one may incline to stand at this juncture of the book.

A Note in Passing

With the seemingly complex global developments been underway at least since when different parts of the world remained no longer remote, and with multiple elements of interaction – social, economic, political, with few evident and several others not, the line of progress of history since then is ever susceptible to this phenomena. Writing history, therefore, is a delicate balance in this atmosphere, and that means the identification of the causation of events in the storyline, part and parcel of the current undertaking, is harder as I mentioned in passing in the Introduction.

Therefore it may appear futile to draw into a study of historical events and identifying a proper chain of causation to them – unencumbered by various other forces of which some may be imperceptible to the probing eye. That is, what appears to be causation between two developments may rightfully end up having zero correlation. Such is the slippery slope in this atmosphere that the writer bounds to make mistakes. In this book, I engage in no small extent upon supreme forces rather than a set of individuals of historical significance. In the efforts to trace the causes of grand developments, the role of specific decisions made by powerful men is circumvented to chase after the few historical and institutional forces. That it is given way instead to exploring and integrating into the story those forces larger and significant than few powerful individuals; forces whose characteristics or origins lay in human nature and human tendencies, economic interest and technological uncertainty, faith and doctrine.

Our discussion of the role of Liberalism navigates those historical events through the eyes of those non-individual forces, and therefore it is only reasonable to study them in more detail in the next two Chapters.

Chapter Two
Nomenclature, Timelines, and Concepts

Timelines

To fully understand the variant forces of polity, industry, and institutions, it is essential to identify the series of phases constituting those forces and represented in such forms respectively as Nation-state, Industry, and Religion, stretching back as long as possible.

Thus, the rise and fall of Nation-state – a geopolitical entity inhabited by people with common identity – across the world in the past two-hundred-and-fifty years is the first factor of concern.

The advent of the Industrial revolution – the period that witnessed spree of inventions and discoveries – is the second factor of concern. To the factor representing this development, I shall merely refer to it as the phenomena of Industry.

The fall of religion, or accurately, the fall of the share of the people of faith in a country within a society is the third factor of concern.

Those three factors being central to the story, the series of phases for each is deconstructed below. The terminology for different Ages beginning with a specific year and ending with another connotes the characteristic feature of it. Thus, when the Nation-state factor is of concern, the terminology and the timeline for various phases is as follows:

First: The Age of Nation-state (1776 – 1975). That is, a period of two-hundred years from the Declaration of

Independence from the British rule in 1776 by the representatives of the thirteen colonies to Britain's successful referendum in 1975 to give consent to joining the Supranational entity, the European Union.

Second: The Late Age of Nation-state (1989 – 1995). That is, the period from the beginning of Soviet disintegration in 1989 to the final culmination in disintegration of the Soviet Federal Republic of Yugoslavia in the form of the Dayton Agreement establishing peace treaty in 1995, marking an end to the Bosnian War.

Third: The Age of Supranational Polity (1976 – 2016). The period from 1976, that is, the year after Britain's full consent to joining the European Union to the successful referendum Vote on Britain's exit from the European Union in 2016.

When the Industry factor is of concern, the terminology and the timeline for various phases is as follows:

First: The Age of pre-Industry (– 1866). That is the period before the advent of the Industrial Revolution.

Second: The Age of Industrial Revolution (1867 – 1913). That is, the period from the invention of Dynamite in 1867 to Ford assembly line sending out Model T in 1913.

Third: The Age of Modernization (1914 – 1973). That is the period from the year after the end of Industrial Revolution to the First Oil Shock following the Arab Oil Embargo in 1973.

Fourth: The Age of Speculation, Expansion, Inversion, and Late Electronics Industry (1974 – 2016). That is the period from the year after the end of Modernization to our present times.

When the Religion factor is of concern, the terminology and the timeline for various phases is as follows:

First: The Age of pre-Darwin (– 1859). That is the period before the publication of Darwin's tome *On the Origin of Species*.

Second: The Age of post-Darwin (1860 – 2017). That is the period after the publication of Darwin's tome *On the Origin of Species* to our present times.

Also, we'll identify the various phases for the following: When Foreign Aggression factor is in play, the terminology and the timeline is as follows:

First: The Age of Colonial Expansion (– 1913). That is the period until the year up to the beginning of the Great War.

Second: The Late Age of Colonial Expansion (1914 – 1945). That is the period from the year of the beginning of the Great War to the end of Second World War.

When the dominance of Liberalism in society – roughly equivalent to the combination of the prominence it gained among the public and to the degree of control it exerted on public opinion – as a factor is of concern, the terminology and the timeline is as follows:

First: The Age of Rise of Liberalism (1914 – 1945). That is the period from the year of the beginning of the Age of Modernization to the end of Second World War.

Second: The Age of Consolidation of Liberalism (1946 – 2016). That is the period since the end of Second World War to US Presidential Election in November 2016.

The following sections each through the end of this Chapter elaborate on few fundamental ideas of economics relevant to the discussion in further Chapters. It is by no means an exaggeration to say that a lot of complexity concerning the discipline of economics evaporates once the structure of real-world economic activity is drawn and laid out. Writing my first book, I developed a framework to understand the intricacies of modern economic activity, and it has come to be extremely useful for that purpose, and now for this book as well. Because a lot of it has to do with the identification and classification of various economic building blocks, the following sections are a more straightforward account of the same, although abridged, to serve appropriately for the purpose at hand.

Classification of Economic Activity by Market

Markets for economic goods can be divided into five distinct groups: primary commodity markets, processed commodity markets, consumer goods markets, final goods heavy industry markets and services markets. All five represent markets of products and services that have economic value. Those five together can be called "Economic Goods markets" in that the production of goods described by all of these markets whether in pre-final form or final are part of the annual gross economic output of a country.

Further, it is important to note that besides the markets of economic goods, there also exist markets of assets, as part of the structure that makes up a capitalist economy. Asset markets represent together all of those markets organized for selling and purchasing of assets already acquired or created before. They primarily are not economic goods created brand new in the current year; instead, they represent an item in one way or another on the balance sheet of the seller or of the purchaser. They are a stock acquired in the past. In contrast, the goods and services that we call economic goods represent items that correspond to the income statement. Thus, Asset markets and Economic Goods markets together make up the capitalist economy; the former corresponds to capital or wealth, and the latter to income. A person buying few shares of a specific company, or buying a house is transacting within Asset markets, whereas purchasing of food, drinks, and clothes fall under Economic Goods markets.

It may be stated that surprisingly many preeminent economists, or the textbooks they write, or even the prominent economic thinkers of the past evident from the economic theories they concocted, failed to recognize this feature that is simple but central to begin to understand the complex and dynamic Capitalist economic system. All too often Economic Goods markets enter the frame of analysis, as given; the subject of Assets markets is dealt under a whole different spotlight and often under Financial Economics. Lost to them is that many answers lie at the intersection of the two markets. Or to state more precisely, the link between balance sheet (assets and debt) and income statement (economic goods) at the individual level or business level prove crucial to understanding transformative events such as the 2008 financial crisis, as we'll see.

Next, we'll discuss classification of economic goods by industry, which is the system of classification based on the kind of economic activity underpinning an economic good as opposed to the just-concluded system of goods classification that was based on degree of development of the good and on a market level. Following this part is a discussion on classification of national capital based on type.

Classification of Economic Activity by Industry

Consider Fig. 2.1. All economic activities – activities that produce economic goods constituting the overall Economic Goods markets – in a modern industrial country can be broken down into the familiar, three strata of the economy: primary industry, secondary industry, and tertiary industry. Primary industry comprises all activities related to agriculture, forestry, and fishing (Section A). Secondary industry is classified further into four sections: mining & quarrying industry (Section B), manufacturing industry (Section C), utility industry {electricity, water, gas, steam and air conditioning supply, waste management} – (Section D, E), and construction industry (Section F). The third one, tertiary industry comprises all services-related industries, which we'll identify at length shortly. The section level ends here. Moving down the classification and below the section level, the manufacturing industry is classified into two divisions: light industry manufacturing and heavy industry manufacturing. Heavy industry manufacturing division itself has two subdivisions namely: upstream industry and final goods heavy industry. Upstream industry comprise the following sectors: 1) Upstream Chemical Industry 2) Upstream Earth Industry 3) Upstream Metals Industry. Further, the Final goods heavy industry has two sectors: 1) Capital Machinery Industry and 2) Capital Equipment Industry.

Services activities include (not shown in the figure): Wholesale and retail trade, repair of motor vehicles and motor cycles (Section G)– the former effectively being an intermediary between consumer goods industry and consumers as shown; Transportation and storage (Section H); Accommodation and food service activities (Section I); Information and communication (Section J); Financial and Insurance activities (Section K); Real estate activities (Section L); Profession, scientific and technical activities (Section M); Administrative and support service services (Section N); Public administration and defense, compulsory social security (Section O); Education (Section P); Human health and social work activities (Section Q); Arts, entertainment and recreation (Section R); Other service activities (Section S); Activities of households as employers, undifferentiated goods-and-services-producing activities of households for own use (Section T); Activities of extraterritorial organizations and bodies (Section U).

Figure 2.1 – Classification of All Economic Activity

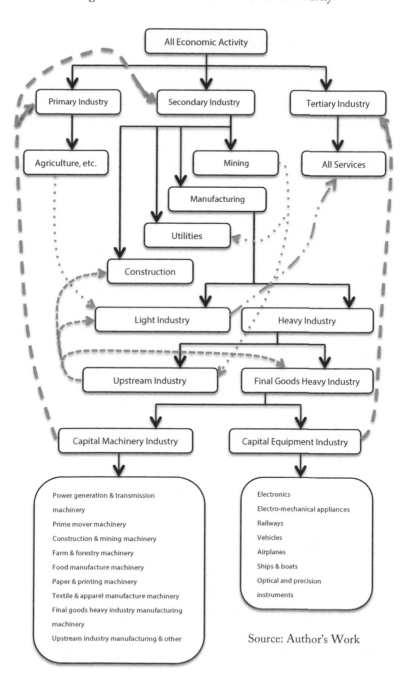

Source: Author's Work

Legend: Primary materials (thin dotted lines)
Processed materials (thick dotted lines)
Consumer goods (combination of dotted and broken line)
Machinery & Equipment (thick broken lines)

The concept of classification of economic activity at the section level (from A to U) totaling 21 altogether is drawn from the United Nations' International Standard Industrial Classification of All Economic Activities (ISIC). The complete standards of ISIC are used by a majority of countries around the world for the collection and reporting of statistics. But down the section-level, all classification (i.e., from division to sub-sector) is the work of the author designed to serve the purpose at hand.

Final goods heavy industry, as the term implies, manufactures products that are final. The other subdivision within the heavy industry – the upstream industry – supplies processed materials down to its sister subdivision – the final goods heavy industry. Some examples of Final goods heavy industry products are: within power generation and transmission machinery: steam turbines, water turbines, gas turbines, internal combustion piston engines, electric motor, electric transformer and jet engines. They all have Faraday's Induction law or the Thermodynamic laws or the Law of energy conservation as the scientific principle underpinning design and operation. Within construction and mining machinery: excavators, bulldozers, etc. Those machines have hydraulic principles at the heart of the heavy-duty operation (besides being equipped with mini-machines such as engines and motors).

Most of the products such as those identified above were invented sometime between 1867 and 1913, that is, during the industrial revolution, in Great Britain, the United States, Germany, Italy, and France, etc. These products in practice operate either in conjunction with other products or become an enclosed but essential element within a larger product, for example, engines and gas turbines being the prime movers of such transportation systems: automobiles, ships, boats, airplanes, railways. Importantly, most of these products (or technologies) to this day remain identical to the original conception – unvarying at the level of operating principle foremost but enhanced in performance.

Mining industry supplies ores and minerals to upstream industry for industrial processing. The upstream industry employs techniques and methods developed during the industrial revolution to transform the primary form of ores and minerals into the usable material of forms and types. The processed materials are transported to final goods heavy industry for manufacture of machinery and equipment that we have identified above (gas turbines, internal combustion piston engines, electric motor, electric transformer, etc.) In standard literature, the industry that manufactures machinery and equipment final goods is called "Downstream industry," but I disperse with that term to employ the much more meaningful term "Final Goods Heavy Industry."

The Final goods heavy industry itself is divided into two sectors namely Capital machinery industry and Capital equipment industry. The former manufactures machinery and supplies its output to all of the other businesses falling under the first two strata of the economy, the primary and secondary industry. It supplies machinery to even itself, as it falls under the provision of secondary industry. The latter manufactures equipment and supplies its output to all of the other businesses that fall under the third strata of the economy, the tertiary industry.

The output of the Capital equipment industry – such as electronics, vehicles, railways, airplanes and optical instruments, as is shown in Fig. 2.1 – is manufactured using the machinery supplied from one of the sub-sector of Capital machinery industry (machine tools). Additionally, the operation of the equipment is powered by the output of another sub-sector of Capital machinery industry that being the Prime mover machinery industry. The engines and motors of prime mover industry power not only vehicles geared for land, sea, and air but also crucially enable the operation of electro-mechanical appliances and optical instruments.

Another significant line of classification of all economic activities, profoundly useful further, is based on technology. All industries from sections to divisions under the prior classification can be grouped under Traditional economic activities and Heavy industry activities. Traditional activities comprise all economic activities, except 'heavy industry' division of manufacturing section, and they are Agriculture, forestry, and fishing (primary industry); mining industry, manufacturing industry (except heavy industry), construction industry & utilities industry (secondary industry); and services (tertiary industry).

Classification of Capital

Classification of capital is essential to understand the nature of capital that is at the heart of the production of the aggregate economic goods in a country in any given year.

National Wealth or National Capital in this book always refers to the net wealth of a nation, and the two terms 'wealth' and 'capital' mean the same. Although on an individual level, the net worth is merely the difference between the value of assets and liabilities at a given time, on a national level the focus turn to ultimate capital – the physical, that is – that underwrite the overall assets and liabilities within a country.

Natural resources that are undeveloped do not comprise capital. Only physical body developed and that which yields income (that is, it can provide economic value) shall constitute capital under the going definition.

National capital is classified into these four types 1) Housing capital, 2) Public infrastructure capital, 3) non-Industrial business capital, 4) Heavy industry business capital.

Consider another way of grouping the various classes of economic activity, this time based on the kind of utility the output of the many industries have. The basis is whether a "good" is readily consumable and perishable, or is the good a machine that can manufacture other goods or can provide service? Simply, the basis for classification here comes down to Capital goods and Consumer goods (and services).

Capital goods are goods whether in the primary form (ores) or processed form (steel) or final form (structures, machinery & equipment) that go into the formation of Housing capital, Public infrastructure capital, non-Industrial business capital and Heavy Industry business capital. All products that are not capital goods and irrespective of whether they are in primary form or processed form or final form that go into consumption and together with all services that also form part of consumption comprise consumer goods. An easy way to distinguish capital goods in the final form of any sort or type from consumer goods is to check with these two necessary conditions: see if the "good" in question does not perish and if it allows the extraction of economic value repeatedly. A yes to these two shall most certainly constitute Capital of some sort. As an example, a house does not perish quickly, and it can provide repeated economic value in shelter everyday.

A point of clarification, there exist a specific range of goods produced by the final goods heavy industry, such as electronics and washing machines, that do not necessarily become capital. Specifically, the electronics, electro-mechanical products, vehicles may be accounted in practice as capital or consumer goods depending on the purpose of installment of them. They all qualify for personal consumption and as well as business asset. On that distinction, these products tracing the lineage to Industrial Revolution or Late Electronics Revolution, therefore, happen to be the only few remarkable ones that had found home in the residential place, apart from business. And most of these final industrial products do not move, except for vehicles that in the usage are among the few types regulated by the state in the form of compulsory registration and licensing for individual operation.

On that note, the Capital goods industries come down to the Final goods heavy industry and Construction Industry, and Consumer goods industries come down to the rest of the industries (All other industries). The Upstream industry itself can be cleaved, for the purpose of clarity, into two sectors each one catering to the final production of capital and consumer goods. That allows those two upstream sectors for classification in the corresponding fashion.

The output of final goods heavy industry is primarily machinery and equipment that is purchased by businesses of all stripes. When bought and installed, and put to work, that output (machinery and equipment) becomes capital that is of non-Industrial business or Heavy Industry business in type. A portion of the output of upstream industry – such as glass, cement, steel, ceramics – when acquired to put to use in construction becomes capital that is of housing or public infrastructure in type. All wealth accumulated, besides land, is the output of, and acquired from, heavy industry and construction industry. Heavy industry exists to create wealth, whether it is to manufacture machinery to make other machinery or materials for construction of housing and buildings. The output of light industry manufacturing – which also comprises food manufacture industry – and the output of farming, forestry and fishing, and of services industry essentially make up on the whole what is generally referred as "consumer goods."

As to the various classes of capital, the non-Industrial business capital is the accumulated capital of office spaces, buildings and skyscrapers for business, stores, warehouses and the machinery and equipment installed inside those structures. This form of capital combined with Housing capital and Public infrastructure capital essentially comprises the capital of all businesses doing business in all of the traditional economic activity.

Heavy Industry business capital comprises the accumulated capital of machine tools, and industrial ovens and furnaces, and the corresponding plants that house them, the warehouses and the office spaces as support infrastructure to the underlying business. This capital broadly constitute machinery that generally is a machine tool upon installation can manufacture other machines; and furnaces and ovens that upon productive use can transform raw materials into processed materials that can then be made available to various industries including final goods heavy industry for purchase. The physical product that makes up the Heavy Industry business capital – broadly, machine tools and furnaces – is the output of the industry that is final goods heavy industry. That is, machines tools such as lathe are manufactured using other machines tools, and therefore they are rightfully referred to as the mother of all machines. By the productive use of heavy Industry business capital, the output – processed materials, machinery, and equipment – is produced. The customers of the output are the businesses that own non-Industrial business capital and the businesses that own the heavy Industry business capital. As noted previously, in the latter case, machines are employed to manufacture other machines.

To distinguish between non-Industrial business capital and Heavy Industry business capital these examples are helpful. In

South Korea, the top companies that provide telecommunication services are SK Telecom, KT Corporation, and LG U plus. The capital owned by the three companies falls under non-Industrial business capital. A portion of that capital is made up of telecommunication networking equipment that was probably supplied by South Korea's top electronics maker Samsung Electronics, whose own capital falls under Heavy industry business capital.

South Korea's top construction company Samsung Construction & Trading Corporation, which built the Petronas Towers in Kuala Lumpur and Burj Khalifa in Dubai, owns capital that falls under non-Industrial business capital. A portion of that capital is made up of construction machinery that was probably supplied by South Korea's construction machinery manufacturer Doosan Infracore, whose own capital falls under Heavy industry business capital.

Doosan Infracore belongs to Doosan Group, which also has its own construction company called Doosan Engineering & Construction whose capital falls under non-Industrial business capital. Here, Samsung Electronics and Doosan Infracore are final goods heavy industries performing industrial activities, whereas SK Telecom, KT Corporation, LG Uplus belong to services industry, Samsung Construction & Trading Corporation and Doosan Engineering & Construction belong to construction industry, performing traditional activities, that is, communication services and construction respectively.

To sum up, all four forms of capital, Housing capital, Public infrastructure capital, non-Industrial business capital, and Heavy industry business capital comprise: either material structures (sourced from upstream industry in the form of cement, glass, ceramics etc.), or machinery & equipment (sourced from final goods heavy industry in the way of engines, turbines, bulldozers).

Figure 2.2 – Nexus Between National Wealth and Economic Activity

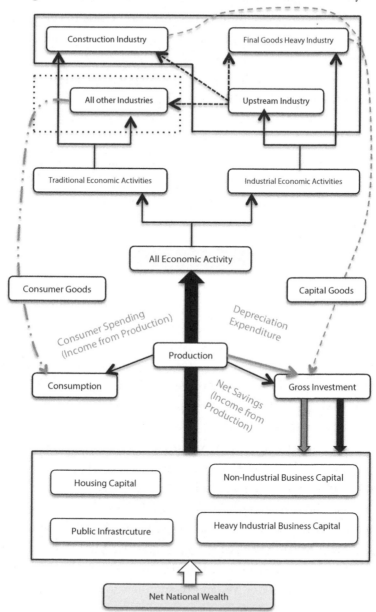

Source: Author's Work

At the core, that is, all forms of wealth or capital accumulation originate from either upstream industry (materials) or final goods heavy industry (machinery and equipment), or together, from Heavy Industry. Now where do consumer goods (and services) come? It is by using machinery and equipment that belongs to non-Industrial business capital accumulated from the output of final goods heavy industry that allows for the manufacture of consumer goods.

As shown in Fig 2.1, Capital machinery industry manufactures machinery that upon installation provides for the performance of activities under primary industry and secondary industry. Capital equipment industry manufactures equipment that upon installation allows for the performance of activities under tertiary industry.

The nexus between the national capital – as classified into four types – and economic activity of all stripes is illustrated in Fig. 2.2. The net National Capital forms the basis for all productive economic activities. At the beginning of a year, the wealth in the starting (say, W_0) allows for a new round of annual production. The income flow originating from this output in the form of wages and profits gets split into income for consumer spending that goes toward the consumption of consumer goods and saving (net) that fund new investment in capital goods (say, equivalent to W_c). Additionally the depreciation expense (say, W_d) that is nobody's income is set aside from the revenue to replenish the wear and tear of the capital stock also chases capital goods. It is the net new capital investment (W_c) and the capital investment (W_d) to replace the depreciated capital that together constitutes gross investment. But the wealth stock at the end of the year becomes $W_0 + W_c$ and in such fashion keeps increasing year-after-year.

All capital goods originate from two industries: construction industry and final goods heavy industry. The upstream industry provides all industries, including the two capital-originating industries, with processed raw materials. The "All Other Industries" includes the industries from Section A to Z, except for the Section F (construction) and the heavy industry division of Section C (manufacturing), and provides with consumer goods and services.

For perspective, consider the net national wealth of the United States, which as estimated by Credit Suisse for their Global Wealth Databook (2015) stands at USD 85.9 trillion in 2015. For the same year, the national income of the US (as calculated by the author using the World Bank data) comes to approximately USD 15.38 trillion. Capital-income ratio for the US at the end of 2015 therefore is 5.58 or 558%. That means for every USD 5.58 of capital, the US economy produced USD 1 of income in 2015. Most Western European countries have capital-income ratios within the higher strata (i.e., 400% and above). Capital-income ratio for a poor country most likely exists below 250%, an evidence of small capital stock possessed by such a country. As a poor country rapidly develops and accumulates capital, capital-income ratio likewise increases year-after-year. As such a country becomes wealthy, the ratio moves beyond 400% and even higher thereafter (due to the asset appreciation caused by speculation on assets, and about which we'll discuss later on).

Economic Development

I have found the following way of understanding the concept of economic development helpful. Simply, economic development through industrialization involves the process of industrialization and modernization. And economic development through non-industrial route involves modernization alone – this route is irrelevant for our purposes, but for those interested: modernization of a country through non-industrial route is achieved on the back of industrialization (and therefore the heavy industry) of foreign countries; heavy industry output is simply imported in this case. Countries of this stripe are Chile, Botswana. Industrialization serves the process of modernization, and the two processes together constitute economic development. Therefore,

Economic development = industrialization + modernization

In the previous section, we have classified capital into four parts: a) Housing capital, b) Public infrastructure capital, c) non-Industrial business capital, d) Heavy Industry business capital. It is the gradual accumulation of Housing capital, Public infrastructure capital and non-Industrial business capital that represent the modernization of all traditional economic activities identified above. And the accumulation of Heavy Industry business capital represents the process of industrialization that serves the above modernization process. Modernization has a definite and useful meaning to it. It refers to the installation of materials, machines, and equipment– all supplied from heavy industry, to perform traditional activities in modern form.

Heavy industry supplies materials such as cement, glass, steel, and machines such as cranes, excavators, and bulldozers for performing construction activity. Heavy industry supplies textile machinery to perform light industry manufacturing of textiles. Heavy industry supplies pulp and papermaking machinery to perform light industry manufacturing of paper and paperboard. Heavy industry supplies power generation machinery such as boilers, turbines and electric generators to enable electricity generation in power plants (utilities). Heavy industry supplies fertilizers and farm machinery to produce agricultural output.

In this way, heavy industry serves to modernize traditional activities. It is the process of industrialization and thus the acquisition of Heavy Industry business capital that enables the economy to produce all of those products listed above, and that supplies materials and machinery & equipment to all traditional economic activities modernizing in the process.

In all early-industrialized countries, industrialization came first instigating modernization. But large-scale and widespread modernization quickened only after the discovery of specific essential processes critical to extraction and manufacturing. The liquefaction of air and Ford's moving assembly line are two such discoveries with profound and far-reaching consequences. About the latter, one such synergy characteristic of inventions at that time was its utterly unanticipated utility in the production of nitrogen for the Haber-Bosch synthesis of Ammonia. Additionally, the discovery of large-scale, steel-making and aluminum-making processes, those being the Bessemer process and Hall-Heroult process respectively, significantly improved the capabilities to supply materials up the value chain in large quantities quickly, enabling large-scale modernization.

A country's drive to accumulate Heavy Industry business capital and in effect enabling the accumulation of housing capital, public infrastructure capital and non-industrial business capital completes the process of economic development through industrialization. The rapid drive of such accumulation of capital in extension represents the process of economic development through *rapid industrialization*. That is a topic of no concern here, and reserved for the discussion of countries that begin industrialization lately.

Classification of wealth into these four forms and especially the classifying of business capital into non-industrial and heavy industry assume importance because it is the process of accumulation of capital of heavy industry businesses that constitutes in effect the industrialization of a country. It is the accumulation of heavy industry business capital that squarely separates industrial nations from non-industrial nations.

Chapter Three
Understanding the Nomenclature

Polity

The characteristic feature of the governing polity across the world – from American declaration of independence to the thousand-year-old independent nation of Great Britain's vote of consent to joining the EU (i.e., from 1776 to 1975) – has been the formulation and emergence of the nation-state in the mold and tradition of the Westphalia system.

The drive toward increasingly greater conflagration among people, eventually resulting in the creation of new national states, or just nation-states is the defining and enduring theme of this period. A nation-state is that system in which people with common identity organize to live within a territory with firm and secure borders and under a single unified polity. The twentieth century spree of nation-state formation emerged from the ashes of the precipitously collapsed colonial enterprise.

The Colonial Age featured two different kinds of empires: the colonial empire, wherein the conquering nation settled the conquered territory, and the trading empire, wherein the purpose was the establishment and the protection of trade routes to pursue protectionist trade with the conquered territory. Colonial empires were confined mainly to the New World, while the trading empires limited to the Old. The five primary colonial powers, Portugal, Spain, Netherlands, France, and Britain all were dual empires.

The Early Age of Discovery (1420-1492) took off with Portugal successfully rounding of the tip of Africa. During the

Late Age of Discovery (1492-1522) both Portugal and Spain achieved considerable success on the Oceans as Christopher Columbus made the journey to the Americas, Vasco de Gama rounding off the Cape of Good Hope to reach India, and Ferdinand Magellan (his crew, in fact) circumnavigating the globe.

Spain and Portugal divided between them the eastern and western hemispheres of the world as Spain settled most of Latin America, with Brazil going to Portugal. On the other side, Spain captured the Philippines, even as Portugal grabbed the neighboring islands.

Following the successes of the Iberian nations, Britain, France, and the Netherlands joined the exploration, launching the Age of Exploration (1522-1775). The French settled into the eastern part of today's Canada and the US, despite fierce competition from the English. The Netherlands controlled exterior portions of the Indonesian islands, while the English colonized Australia and New Zealand; and these five naval powers conquered various Caribbean islands, establishing trading posts along the coasts of Africa and India. India itself fell into the hands of Britain as the latter sought increasing monopolization of trade with the subcontinent. During this period, Russia expanded into the Siberian hinterlands, thereby successfully establishing the Russian Empire.

The Age of Transition (1776-1913) oversaw three new developments: the dissolution of the control held by the European powers in the New World; the expansion and the consolidation of European control in Asia, including India; and the Scramble for Africa. The American Revolutionary War, the Latin American Wars of Independence (1810-1830), the latter sparked by Napoleon's occupation of Spain coupled with the destabilization of power on the Spanish throne, culminated into the first significant wave of modern nation-states formation

Figure 3.1 – Number of New Nation States Created 1816 – 2000

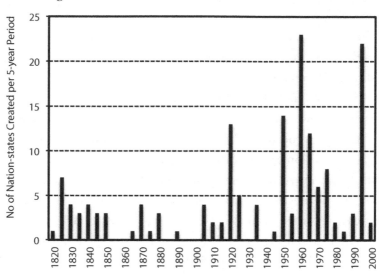

Source: Andreas Wimmer & Yuval Feinstein, "The Rise of the Nation-State across the World, 1816 to 2001," *American Sociological Review*, 2010, vol. 75, no. 5, pp. 764–790

outside Europe, as shown in Fig 3.1. The Wars of Independence wrecked the Spanish empire. With the passage of British North America Act in 1867, Canada was declared a dominion within the British Empire, establishing the territory as a self-governing entity. During this period, the US emerged as the predominant power in the New World. At the turn of the twentieth century after the Spanish-American War, the Spanish empire succumbed at last as Cuba came out of the war as a republic in 1902 with the Philippines and Puerto Rico ceded to the US.

As the New World slipped, expansion and consolidation of European control in Asia (1820-1880) captured interest as Britain, France, Russia and the Netherlands vastly expanded the territory of their empires. Britain controlled South Asia, including British India (1857), Myanmar (1826, 1852) and Malaysia (1824), while France gradually conquered Indo-china

(Vietnam, Laos, Cambodia), Russia expanded eastward and southward, as only Thailand evaded conquest. Britain forced China into economic imperialism; the Asian country had to sign lopsided trade agreements in the aftermath of the Opium Wars and to hand over the island of Hong Kong to Britain.

Scramble for Africa (1880-1913) was the fight among the European powers for the occupation, division, and colonization of the African continent. Britain and France dominated the drive for African colonization. Britain seized the wide strip of territory from Egypt down to South Africa, while France took control of most of the western part of the continent. The five secondary participants in the scramble were Spain, Portugal, Belgium, and the newly united Germany and Italy. The occupation was swift as ninety percent of the continent came under the European control by 1913 when only ten percent of the continent was under control as early as 1870.

The African continent, after the initial contacts and setup of few trading posts and ports of call by the Portuguese along the coastline during the Age of Discovery, was left mostly unexplored for another two centuries. The early to mid-eighteenth century expeditions of David Livingstone, H.M. Stanley helped map the interiors; Livingstone explored Southern Africa, while Stanley explored Central Africa. Further expeditions in the 1850s and 1860s by Richard Burton, John Speke, and James Grant helped identify the Great Central lakes and the source of the Nile.

Africa's endowment of vast mineral wealth lured the European powers especially in times of economic distress to launch several African expeditions during the mid-century. The demand for raw materials that were unavailable in Europe, especially copper, cotton, rubber, palm oil, cocoa, diamonds, tea, and tin, had skyrocketed since the dawn of the Industrial

Revolution. African expeditions seemed to offer a way out to fill the short gap in raw materials.

By the 1870s, Portugal controlled the present-day Angola and Mozambique, whereas Britain and France took the Cape Colony and Algeria respectively. By 1914, except for Ethiopia and Liberia, the entire African continent came under the control of European powers.

By 1910, Western colonization of the Old World was so complete that few countries remained outside the purview of the European powers. Thus, the Age of Colonial Expansion (– 1913), marked the latter's end (1913) before a grand conflict broke out in the fight over the possessions that were acquired until then.

At the turn of the twentieth century, the colonies acquired by Western powers of France and Britain soon came under challenge from the rising power Germany. The struggle between the consolidating powers and the emerging powers over the distribution of prior colonial spoils launched what may be called the Late Age of Colonial Expansion (1914 – 1945) – the period from the beginning of Great War to the end of Second World War.

The collapse of Ottoman Empire, Austro-Hungarian Empire, Romanov Empire, during the Great War and in the aftermath, gave in to the second wave of the formulation of new nation-states, as shown in from Fig 3.1. The colonies in the Old World also gained independence after the Second World War, as British, French, and Japanese Empires crumbled; Portuguese possessions in Africa, and Dutch control over Indonesia and Western New Guinea slipped. This development resulted in the third wave of the formulation of new nation-states, as many countries in South Asia, East Asia, and Africa gained sovereignty.

In the Age of Nation-state, the number of new nation-states created from the disintegration of various age-old polities, such as empires, colonies, island port-hubs, or from the integration of the small and large princely kingdoms, duchies, provinces, accelerated throughout the most part of the early and mid-twentieth-century, as is clear in Fig 3.1.

The three waves of new nation-state formulation – the first wave after the Latin American Wars of Independence, the second after the First World War, and the third wave just after the Second World War – had drastically altered the geopolitical landscape across the world over time. The direction was toward the creation of a geopolitical entity 'the state' for people with common identity away from large empire-style polities.

What may be called the fourth wave, the Late Age of Nation-state is a result, directly, of the delayed disintegration of the Russian empire, which after the Russian Civil War (1917 – 1921) had morphed into a monolithic federation, the Union of Soviet Socialist Republics (USSR).

The drive toward the formation of nation-state – a system in which people with a common identity organize to live within a defined border and form a governing polity – and the sustainment of it can be construed to be the normality, as evidenced from the spree of creation of two hundred plus of the same illustrated over a stretch of time in Fig 3.1.

In a nation-state, peoples' connection to each other transcends religion and ethnicity, which means under this banner a country like China and India with many number of ethnicities and religious affiliations living together identify as one, and nominally reflect shared values. In the simplest terms, these people coming to live together under a state agree on few basic principles that their shared beliefs outweigh their differences, at least to the extent that a written constitution can be drafted. This national culture is often reinforced and achieved through a common language, history, education, and holidays. Specifically, a nation-state is a system of political, geographic, and cultural organization, held together by people connected to each other by a firm boundary and by a single government.

By having the member states relinquishing a part of the national sovereignty, the Age of Supranational polity is the period in which the trans-national, or trans-continental bodies emerged as the elite, standard-mode of conducting the business of politics. These bodies assigned and empowered with a variety of missions and powers, in our present times quite astonishingly and surreptitiously, have had magnified into behemoth physical and legal entities, such as the United Nations, the European Union, the International Monetary Fund, the World Bank, etc.

Industry

The marked break from prehistory to history, or from the hunter-gatherer tribal lifestyle to agricultural societies was a development primarily caused by a change of relationship among the people, and between the people and nature. The fruits of nature in one form or another have been available to planet Earth's inhabitants for exploitation since time immemorial. Given that, the break in the way of life and work was due to the change in the method, or manner, or form, or extent, or speed of exploitation, rather than the change in the endowment from nature per se. In the same vein, the advent of Industrial Revolution was such a marked break away from the then agrarian and traditional way of life. Quite apparently, the characteristic feature wrought due to the advent and spread of the revolution has been the rapid and enhanced method of exploitation of nature's resources.

The Age of pre-Industry was marked by little and slow exploitation of nature's materials and energy. Thus, all traditional economic activities including farming, forestry, and fishing (primary industry), mining, light manufacturing, energy, water, construction (secondary industry), services (tertiary industry) were performed in a pre-industrial manner. That is, the activities were characterized, to the modern eye, by their astronomical reliance on labor, land, and animals.

Fig 13.1 (in Chapter 13) represents the aggregate world GDP growth rate since 1 AD to 2003. The near-zero growth rate of the aggregate economic activity all the way up to the early-nineteenth-century, and about half-percent growth rate mainly across the West in the fifty years before the advent of the Industrial Revolution illustrate the stagnant nature in the speed of exploitation of nature's resources until 1820. It further highlights how this growth picked up pace due to the spread of the early inventions such as steam engine and bogie, and the early textile machinery.

The Age of Industrial Revolution (1867-1913) changed everything. The relationship between man and nature underwent a dramatic transformation, leading to an earth-shattering effect, perhaps quite literally, when Alfred Nobel invented the explosive Dynamite as a safer alternative to gunpowder in 1867.

The year 1867 also marked the introduction of the first practical designs of the dynamo and the open-hearth steel-making furnaces and the definite formulation of the second law of thermodynamics. The year 1913, bringing to an end the Age of Industrial Revolution, marked the introduction of the first continuously moving assembly line at the Ford Company that had since revolutionized mass production, and the successful commercialization of Haber-Bosch ammonia synthesis, without which the world would not have been able to feed billions, and lastly the invention of Kaplan water turbine.

Figure 3.2 – Spree of Inventions During the Industrial Revolution

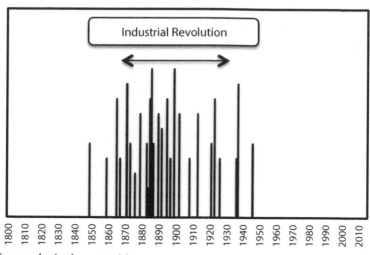

Source: Author's composition

Each bar representing an invention for that specific year, the list of inventions that had given origin to each new sub-sector within the final goods heavy industry as illustrated in Fig 3.2 are: water turbine 1849; electric storage battery 1859; universal milling machine 1865; electric generator 1867; telephone 1871; automatic screw machine 1873; universal grinding machine 1876; light bulb 1879; electric elevator 1883; steam turbine 1884; internal combustion engine, combine harvester 1885; transformer 1886; A/C electric motor, dish washer, gear hobbing machine 1887; tractor 1890; diesel engine 1892; automatic lathe 1895; high-precision grinding machine 1896; hydraulic excavator 1897; refrigerator 1899; air conditioner 1902; washing machine 1908; Kaplan water turbine 1913; jig borer 1921; bulldozer 1923; rocket engine 1926; cotton picker 1936; gas turbine 1937; microwave oven 1946.

Fig 3.2 also illustrates the synergy and the output of the Industrial Revolution drawn on the two-hundred-and-fifteen-year timeline from 1800 to 2015. The year of the invention of the technologies, which upon commercialization, and upon diffusion of those technologies to other Western countries, had effectively launched the final goods heavy industry and also launched each of the industry sub-sector that comprise final goods heavy industry.

The pace of invention during the period between 1867 and 1913 accelerated. With the advent of Great War, the delayed inventions such as Jig Borer (1921)– used in heavy industry manufacturing technology, bulldozer (1923), rocket engine (1926), cotton picker (1936), gas turbine (1937), were promptly invented and integrated into the economic system before, during and after the breakout of the next major war, the Second World War.

The Age of Modernization (1914 – 1973) is a continuation, but somewhat in the speediest terms, of the modernization of every other traditional economic activity. Supplanted with the machinery and material from heavy industry manufacturing division– the division that came into existence with the advent of the Industrial Revolution, within the manufacturing section that with among other sections of industry make up the totality of national economic activity.

The Age of Modernization came to a halt in 1973 as the Arab oil embargo spiked oil prices causing inflation and plummeting investment. There was a precipitous decline in the aggregate new investment undertaken every year in Western countries since modernization ended. This phenomenon is gleaned from Fig 3.3 showing French national savings as percent of national income each year from 1820 to 2010, except for these two periods: the Franco-Prussian war (1871 and 1872), and the crisis years of World Wars and Depression (1915 to 1944). The trend is similar in the other three major western economies, the UK, the US, and Germany (See Figure 12.1 in Chapter Twelve for US savings rate). The case of France is critically essential here

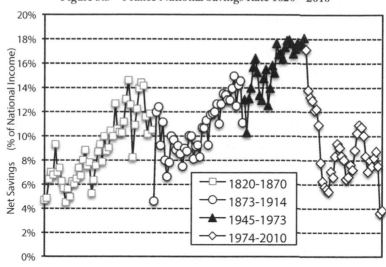

Figure 3.3 – France National Savings Rate 1820 – 2010

Source: Alvaredo Facundo, Anthony B. Atkinson, Thomas Piketty, Emmanuel Saez, & Gabriel Zucman, *The World Wealth and Income Database* 2016 <http://www.wid.world>

because it is for this country that we have data on savings rate stretching back the longest, going back even before Industrial revolution came along.

For France, and even for West Germany, besides the continuing modernization process, the postwar years were characterized by reconstruction and re-accumulation of capital lost and destroyed during the prior wars and foreign occupation. That is why savings rate in the postwar years has been historically higher as compared to the subdued rates before it for both France and Germany.

As for the UK and the US, the savings rate in the postwar era enjoyed historically higher figures reflecting rapid modernization of those times including spending on public infrastructure such as interstate highways, and suburban housing and intra-city connectivity. But the rates for the two countries remained below that of France and Germany in large part because the two Anglo-Saxon countries did not see foreign invasion during the Second World War.

The Age of Speculation, Expansion, Inversion, and Late Electronics Industry (1974 – 2016) marked by the breakaway from the past in the form of the end of modernization, after having exhausted the opportunities presented from industrialization and modernization, led in effect to an alternative means of wealth accumulation and for the provision of investment returns.

Although there have been many noteworthy speculative busts over the past four-hundred-years, speculation of capital is a distinctive feature of this Age, mainly due to two reasons. First, the spectrum of capital assets was varied and diverse, unlike previously. Speculative investments could be executed on any form of capital, including housing capital. Second, the size of the aggregate wealth (the net-worth) attained by the Western countries on a per-capita basis or even on a capital-income ratio (aggregate national capital/annual national income) basis remained high.

It is because of the advent of the Industrial Revolution and the modernization of the traditional economic activities that there existed a considerable size and spectrum of capital available for speculation. Often vast fortunes demand increasingly higher returns, or to put it accurately, wield the capacity to muster resources to procure higher returns, i.e., returns of 3% to even 10%, and with the gains themselves being substantial enough and proportionate to the fortune, the concentration of the wealth spirals faster and faster.

The expansion and the inversion of capital in this Age is simply the result of a drive towards reduction of operating costs by corporate business by inverting manufacturing to low-wage, labor-abundant, overseas locations, and of an incessant lookout

Figure 3.4 – Late Electronics Revolution 1947 – 1973

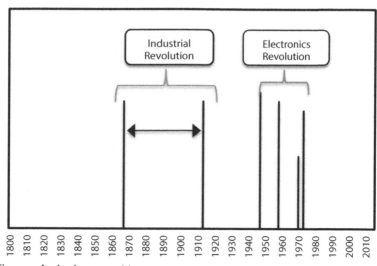

Source: Author's composition

for the expansion and the enlargement of market(s) that serve to boost revenue, year-after-year, decade-after-decade, to meet the Wall Street-demanded quarterly profit targets.

Fig 3.4 illustrates the advent of the Late Electronics Revolution (1947 – 1973), in which each bar represents an invention for that specific year, with the inventions of the transistor (1947), integrated circuit (1958), computer mouse (1970), and graphical user interface (1973). The lateness of these inventions compared to those of the Industrial Revolution was due to the lagged development of the science it relied on, or more precisely, due to the time lag incurred to fully see the development of twentieth-century particle physics as the successor to the nineteenth-century classical physics. That has affected the course of events, primarily, in two ways.

First, in the Age of Speculation, Expansion, and Inversion – that is, the Age succeeding the previous two Ages that allowed for direct wealth accumulation on the top of industrialization and modernization – the electronics revolution opened up the last cusp for immediate and direct wealth accumulation through an undertaking of new investment in the productive industry. That development had given in to the Late Electronics Industry– the commercialization and the application and development of the breakthroughs from Late Electronics Revolution. Hence the massive tech-bubble that manifested itself in the March 2000 NASDAQ peak. We'll return to this topic later on. Second, the Late Electronics Industry made possible the centralization of the new communication platforms, which have on its ascent to dominance destroyed the old school, decentralized systems of communication.

Religion

In the Age of pre-Darwin, a dominant share of the people of religious faith had characterized the Western society.

In the Age of post-Darwin or the period after the publication of Darwin's masterpiece *On the Origin of Species*, the steady decline of the share of the people of religious faith, from very little initially for a few decades, accelerated during the Age of Modernization and continued apace.

According to Gallup Poll, in 1937 – the year this specific poll began – 73% Americans among the surveyed had a positive response when asked whether they happen to be a member of a church, synagogue, or mosque. The figure, as seen in Fig 3.5, remained steady in the subsequent polls until the mid-1970s when it began an uneven decline hitting 65% in the late-1980s. Since the turn of the millennium, the decline quickened, as the figure hit an all-time low of 54% in 2015.

To another Gallup poll question in 1955 as to whether they happened to attend a church, synagogue or mosque in the last seven days or not, 49% respondents answered affirmatively (the

Figure 3.5 – Share of Respondents Who Claimed Membership in Religious Institutions

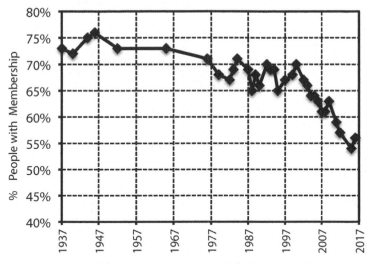

Source: Five Key Findings on Religion in the US, Gallup Poll, December 2016

figures remained jumbled from 1938 to 1950). This number in the subsequent polls declined to 40% by the mid-1970s and after that continued uneven, with ups and down around the 42% figure. Only 36% respondents answered yes to the same question in 2016.

Turning to the question of the importance of religion in one's own life, 70% respondents in the 1965 poll chose the answer "very important" (other choices included fairly important, not very important). This number, as seen in Fig. 3.6, declined to 52% by 1978 and has since then remained within the confines of the 50%–60% bracket. In the latest poll conducted in 2016, the figure remained at 53%. In the very same year, only 22% said religion was fairly important and a whopping 25% not very important. In contrast, just 12% identified religion not very important in 2000 – a figure that had remained almost stable since 1992 up to then.

Figure 3.6 – Share of Respondents Who Viewed Religion Very Important

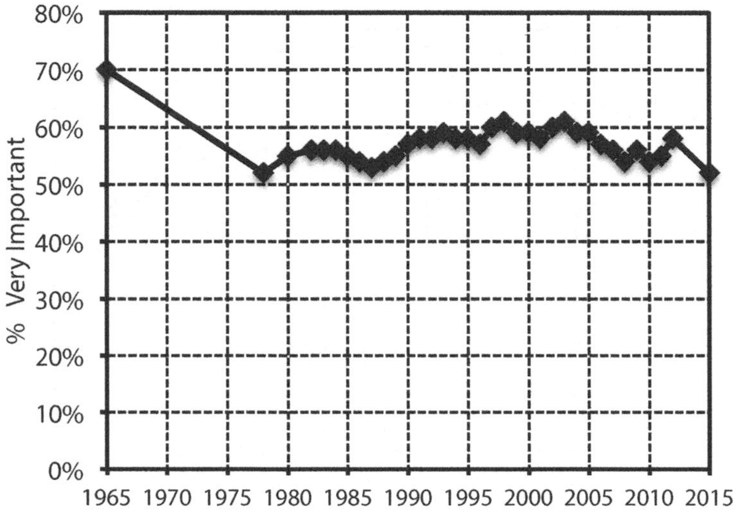

Source: Five Key Findings on Religion in the US, Gallup Poll, December 2016

In 2016, 72% of surveyed Americans perceived that religion is losing its influence on American life – a figure that has remained constant in the past eight years. In a May 2017 poll, only 38% of the respondents believed in the Creationist view of humans – a figure lower than at any point in Gallup's history on that question. In a May 2017 Gallup poll regarding the belief in the existence of God, 64% said they were convinced God exists, 16% said "probably exists, have a little doubt," another 5% said "probably does not exist, but have a lot of doubt," a further 6% said, "probably does not exist, but not sure," while another 7% said, "convinced God does not exist," and lastly, about 2% had no opinion.

In 2016, the Southern states remain the most religious, with Mississippi (59%) leading the pack followed by Alabama (56%), Utah (54%), South Dakota (53%), South Carolina (52%), Arkansas (52%), Louisiana (50%), Tennessee (59%), Oklahoma

(49%), Georgia (47%), North Carolina (47%), and Kentucky (47%). Vermont (21%) heads the list of least religious states followed by Maine (23%), Massachusetts (25%), Rhode Island (27%), Nevada (27%), Alaska (27%), Oregon (27%), Connecticut (28%), Hawaii (28%), New Hampshire (29%), Washington (29%).

Among the wealthy nations, the United States stands alone in its embrace of religion. According to Pew Research Center report, more than half of Americans (53%) in 2015 say religion is very important in their lives. This figure declined from 59% in 2002, and 56% in 2007. As per the report, people in wealthier nations tend to place less importance on religion than those in poorer nations, with the US being a notable exception to this observation. Americans are much more likely than people in other wealthier advanced countries to say religion is very important. Going by this trend, in 2015 among the wealthy nations Japan took the lowest spot with only 11% reporting that religion was very important in their lives, which was followed by France (14%), Australia (18%), South Korea (19%), UK (21%), Spain (21%), Germany (21%), Italy (26%), Canada (27%), Chile (27%), and Israel (34%). Globally, countries with communist-past appear at the lowest rung of this list, prominently China (3%) at the bottom (with Japan following it), while Russia at 19% took sixth place.

Countries such as Ethiopia (98%), Senegal (97%), Indonesia (95%), Uganda (94%), Pakistan (93%), Burkina Faso (92%), Tanzania (90%), Ghana (90%), Nigeria (88%), Philippines (87%), Kenya (86%), Malaysia (84%), Jordan (83%), India (80%), Palestinian territory (74%), Brazil (74%), South Africa (67%), Peru (66%), Lebanon (57%), and Turkey (56%) appear at the upper end of the list as it comes to the question of importance of religion in one's daily life. Evidently, African and South Asian nations feature at the upper echelon, whereas the wealthy western and Pacific, ex-communist countries at the lower one. A significant exception to this trend, as noted already, is the United States.

According to the latest Pew Research Center report, of Oct 2017, most US adults now say it is not necessary to believe in God to be moral and have good values (56%), a figure that has gone up from 49% in 2011. Although the polling data does not encapsulate the full picture, it nevertheless provides a perspective from which the trend of decline, and if so, how fast, may be assessed.

Thus far we have become familiar with the terminology for the various phases of the three significant factors of concern – the nation-state, industry, and religion. We have also examined the characteristic features of the different timespans within the timeline of each phase.

Chapter Four
Fallout from Nineteenth Century Liberalism

The Self-regulating Market

In this Chapter, we'll cover the causes of some of the major events occurred between the early to mid-twentieth century – the First World War, the Russian Revolution, the Paris Peace Conference, the rise of Communism and Fascism, and the Second World War.

The fallout from nineteenth-century Liberalism–meaning the secondary or lingering effects, or rather, the set of consequences, had precipitated the above twentieth century disasters. As such, the set of forces that brought the first significant debacle, the Great War, lay far into nineteenth century and beyond.

The new nation-states created from the ashes of the collapsing colonial enterprise from early to mid-twentieth century across the world – a follow-up to the nation-state polity spree from the previous century – witnessed one significant divergence in the form of the delayed disintegration of the Russian Empire.

After the Second World War, the Russian Empire, having embarked upon the implementation of a pseudo-scientific theory of socio-economic activity previously, had then gobbled up large portions of the world into its sphere of control instead of displaying tendencies of breaking down to new nation-states, like other empires. However, the divergent path of the Russia Empire inevitably tended toward disintegration and breakup and to the emergence of nation-states carved out of the republics within it.

The question persists as to the emergence of the ideology that fused together the Party and animated its leaders in the Soviet Union. To do that we have to go back to the origins to explore the ultimate causes of the tectonic shifts rippling through Europe. It was Europe that found a place for such an ideology, whose implementation in the USSR had produced a surreal display of totalitarian control of society and the individual, and had further magnified the danger through its streak of victories in the efforts to spread the ideology bent on total world control.

Having embarked on that task, we have to go back to the eighteenth century Great Britain that was home for everything revolutionary– to the mind of men from the Middle Ages, including the idea of modern revolutions. The economic front of Liberalism strictly believed in the laissez-faire principle. On this as on others, Liberalism's sharp and clear standing on the matters of economy and state had invariably affected the course of events beyond the pure capital-labor consternation raging among the political economists and philosophers at the time in Britain.

Laissez-faire policy during the entire nineteenth century, led in its implementation by Great Britain and followed by France and the US, had come to be seen as the ideal mechanism to grow the economy and create wealth. That in practice had meant implementing the grossly erroneous notion of the Self-regulating market. Throughout the century, the Liberal doctrine posited that Adam Smith's invisible hand does a better job regulating the market; the state's role, at the most, is to protect private property and the corresponding wealth created from economic activity; any state intervention in the market distorts market outcomes.

As it came to state involvement in the economy, liberalism preached polemically, and somewhat naively that "the laissez-faire economy" was the ideal policy on the part of the state. The message was loud and clear: the state should stay out of the market economy.

Over the nineteenth century the ideas of laissez-faire economics – embedded in any of these phrases "laissez-faire economy," "Self-regulating market," "laissez-faire economics-guided state" with some notable exceptions in the western hemisphere dominated the state policy. But as soon as the state went along the laissez-faire direction, it immediately resorted to enacting suitable measures to curtail the consequences arising from the system. That, in fact, was what transpired through that century and all the way until the outbreak of the Great War.

However even as the state began to look for protective measures, Liberalism's simple laissez-faire economics had sown the seeds for the emergence of a climate of divergence. In addition, this was a development coinciding with the era of tectonic shifts caused by the advent of Industrial Revolution. The resulting chaos had durably provided adequate momentum to undertake a profound examination of the then prevailing economic system that we today identify as Capitalism with far-reaching consequences.

But first, it is essential to understand why the idea of "Self-regulating market" is such a false proposition, and what may be the consequences of implementing it.

The variety of raw materials, workforce, technology and others that go into economic activity or the three strata of the Industry on the surface obey the fundamental law of supply and demand of the market in the strictest sense, except for these three: land, labor, and money. As it comes down to these three commodities, the law of supply and demand falls flat only because the supply of any of the three cannot be increased in a sovereign nation after seeing a demand increase for it. In other words, that is, they are the fictitious commodities of the market besides the fact that the three are also the most significant foundations of national economy.

Life is an indelible component of Labor that is not produced upon an increase in the demand for labor; Land being the inextricable part of nature again not produced for sale. Money merely being purchasing power comes to life through the mechanism of the fractional reserve banking system; money cannot be produced in the strictest sense of the term. It was with the assumption that the three elements have the nature of commodity that their markets have been established to build the market economic system.

In England, since creating the market system from the national markets for land, labor, and money, the laissez-faire-guided state intervened into the economy to mainly contain the effects arising from it. The state tried to intervene in the market operations by enacting sweeping legislations. The child labor prohibition laws, the working hours restriction laws, the workplace safety measure laws, laws regulating the relationship between employer and labor – Mines Act of 1842, the Textile Factory Act 1844, the Factories Act of 1847, the Mines Act of 1860, Employers and Workmen Act of 1875, etc. Protecting the labor through the enactment of these regulations in Britain was a step in the direction of containing the effects of having a competitive labor market.

Liberalism's advocacy of the laissez-faire economy did not end with the domestic market (therefore what I referred to as "Self-regulating market" until now is "Self-regulating domestic market," and I continue to employ the former carrying the same meaning). The doctrine's blunt advocacy of laissez-faire extended to the international sphere as well. Therefore the global trade since mid-nineteenth century had come to rely extensively upon the monetary system called the International Gold Standard and to that we turn to next.

The International Gold Standard

The International Gold Standard – a creation of the mid-nineteenth century trans-Atlantic finance – had been the monetary system that enabled international trade among countries by way of payment in Gold. And it had ever since greased foreign trade and investment, acting as the primary mechanism for exports, imports, and capital flow in the Age of Industrial revolution so long as the trading nations consented to the system.

The Self-regulating market and international trade conducted based on the International Gold Standard acted as the epicenters of domestic and international exchange. The Self-regulating market itself was the arbitrating regulator of the monetary system of the International Gold Standard as it came to each country, in conjunction with other trading partners operating along the similar lines.

The Gold Standard, in theory, is a monetary system that allows paper money to be freely convertible to a fixed amount of gold. Given that, paper money's value derived only from having the gold as its ultimate backing. The International Gold Standard system is merely an extension of this concept from domestic to international sphere to facilitate trade. That is, paper money or the domestic currency of a country served as payment for international trade, provided that the domestic currency was backed by a fixed amount of gold that was free to flow in and out of that country without restrictions. Since paper money backed by gold was deemed "as good as gold," the problem of exchange – that which existed due to lack of trust among trading partners on the viability of domestic currency for international payments – had been solved.

That had meant all countries that were part of the International Gold Standard had to follow or adopt these two rules. First, each country would set the value of the domestic currency about a fixed amount of gold that was freely convertible. Second, the domestic money supply would be based on the quantity of gold that country held in its reserves. The adherence to these two rules allowed a country to participate freely in international trade and invest based on this monetary system, that is only if the country allowed free movement of gold inside and outside the country.

In theory, this monetary system of international trade was a self-regulating mechanism on a global scale in the similar vein of the Self-regulating market in the domestic sphere. If a country is sliding towards a deficit, the net outflow of gold to clear payments to international customers will drain the gold reserves of that country. This effect automatically shrinks the domestic money supply and causes interest rates to rise, price levels and wage levels to fall. That entails a declining demand for imports and more competitive exports, a net drive toward a balance of the accounts, and hence self-regulating.

Central banks usually intervened to accelerate the system's self-regulating adjustment process by using discount rate – the rate at which central bank lends money to a commercial bank. It was the go-to tool to influence market interest rates, thereby being able to cool down domestic demand for goods. The modest fall in price levels due to falling domestic demand decreases imports and makes exports competitive; higher interest rates, also, lure foreign investors that in turn improve the capital account position.

The Gold Standard first came into operation in Britain (1821), and many Western countries followed suit most actively from 1850. With Germany joining the system in 1871, many other countries were drawn to it. The United States entered in

1879 but remained bi-metallic (gold and silver that is, but in practice silver coins dwindled long before it joined) until the turn of the twentieth century when Congress passed the Gold Standard Act, making the gold dollar the official unit of currency. By 1900, most countries, with notable exceptions such as China, were part of the system.

For our purposes, the most vivid and enduring aspect of this system comes down to this. Paper money's free on-demand convertibility into gold strictly limited the amount of paper money (essentially, fiat money, that is in the absence of gold backing) in circulation to a multiple of the gold reserves held by central banks. Falling gold reserves over a stretch of time, without a quick adjustment process in place, meant shrinking money supply in circulation, and therefore a general fall in the price level. Deficit countries were especially prone to these forces of deflation that turned out to be inherent to the system itself. While surplus countries could suppress the effects of inflation by restricting credit, the outcome of a shrinking money supply in deficit countries was inevitable so long as that country remained on the system.

Figure 4.1 shows dollar inflation for the United States from 1870 to 2015. From 1834 the yellow metal became the principal form of currency in the US, replacing silver. The US briefly abandoned gold exchange and resorted to fiat money with no convertibility into silver, gold, or any other metal during the Civil War. As it is clear from the figure, inflation and deflation cycles were a standard feature until the US exited the Gold Standard in 1933. Since then only dollar inflation had been a rampant menace to the value and stability of the currency. Large deflationary spirals, one such in the aftermath of the recession during 1921, and another during the Great Depression, when

Figure 4.1 – US Dollar Monthly Inflation Change from 12 Months

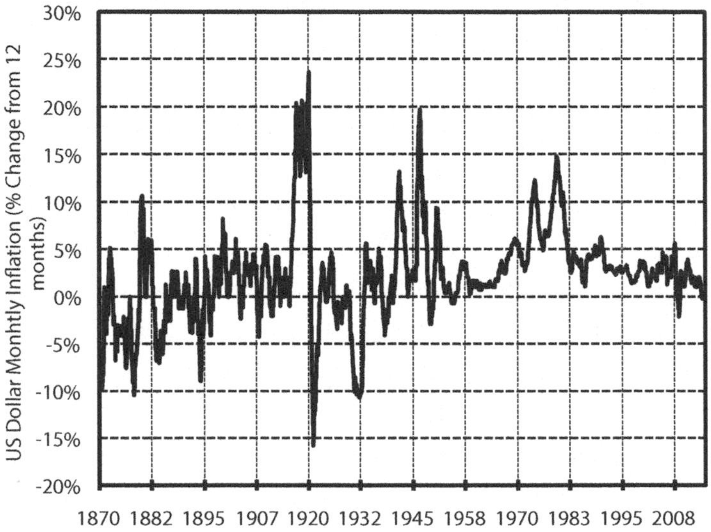

Sources: A) Data for 1870 – 1913: *National Bureau of Economic Research*, Index of the General Price Level for United States, Percent Change from Year Ago, Monthly, Not Seasonally Adjusted; B) Data for 1914 – 2015: *Bureau of Labor Statistics*, CPI-All Urban Consumers (Current Series, 12-Monthly Change, Not Seasonally Adjusted)

the rates essentially fell by 15% and 10% respectively before revving back up.

The International Gold Standard system contained inherent forces of domestic price deflation. A falling price level by extension affects income, savings, outstanding debt (in real terms), and interest payments (in nominal terms) of all parties engaged in domestic economic activity within a country. That was a system that was explosive. From a technical standpoint, the International Gold Standard appears to be, at its best, an unstable system that temporarily greases daily economic activity, and at its worst, a ticking time bomb. With stability being the characteristic feature of the monetary system of the present era it should not, therefore, be surprising to see that we do not have International Gold Standard or any other system of trade resembling one that has Gold acting as an ultimate value backing the exchange money.

However, our present conditions are as they are because of the transformative corrections that were taken at the Bretton Woods conference just before the Second World War ended. The US dollar replaced Gold as the ultimate value. It was the dollar that was valued at the fixed amount of gold that then began to be used as the ultimate exchange money for conducting international trade and investment. Foreign currencies were valued in US dollar – the dollar essentially backing foreign currencies. This system endured and collapsed in 1971 and after which the fiat dollar became the standard means of exchange.

But before the entire World and the West left the Gold Standard for good, the lack of a mechanism to counter the deflationary forces caused by having the dual system of the Self-regulating market and the International Gold Standard – that especially in the Age of Industrial revolution – proved too costly. That is the combination of the Self-regulating market and the International Gold Standard – the crux of laissez-faire economics – had let off forces to produce directly and indirectly few such extraordinary world-scale events.

The Late Scramble for Colonies

The apparent failures of the laissez-faire economy including that of the International Gold Standard in the later part of the nineteenth century across the West, and in addition the scintillating and captivating flair of writing by Karl Marx– who was less than rigorous in his analysis of Capitalism and who, instead of devising a workable course-corrective state-policy, went on to the theorizing of and the realization of an extremely radical, utopian dream of state-controlled economic activity, had enraged and engaged respectively the minds of young insurgents and revolutionaries. They had sought to nullify the results of Capitalism by embarking on the mission to bring the means of production under state control. The first part was the problem; the second was the solution; the former resulted from the utopian heaven, the latter the same.

Thus, in the Age of Industrial revolution the Self-regulating market that partly includes the three fictitious commodities of land, labor, and money, in conjunction with the International Gold Standard, had produced the deflationary spirals in the domestic prices impacting just about every other commodity and their value, including the other two, land & labor. Even as many labor laws enacted to protect labor from market forces, the deflationary spirals affecting the prices of everything including wages created exorbitant social costs. Additionally, the surging and falling unemployment rates were a reflection of the ebb and flow of consequences of having the Self-regulating market and the International Gold Standard. And it was the persisting unemployment and vanishing savings and rising debt payments that had born out to impact the economies of the industrial West, especially disastrously in the aftermath of the Great Depression, as we'll see.

Even the market price of land could not have escaped the indirect deflationary forces, as in the price of debt incurred by an individual to accumulate a plot of land. For example, at the beginning of the year, the outstanding debt incurred in the acquisition of a piece of land is, say, USD 1000 with a fixed monthly bank payment sum of, say, USD 20 that amounts to one-fifth of the debtor's monthly income of USD 100. But the falling prices over the course of the year means that the debtor still has to pay the same fixed monthly sum of USD 20. That effectively ends up to having to pay more in real value out of the supposedly constant real monthly-income stream, which had now fallen by the end of the year, say, to a nominal value of USD 80 – shelling out now about one-fourth to clear the debt.

As the disastrous outcomes of the market system came to the fore, the laissez-faire-economics-guided state looked out for colonies for preferable trade to counter, or to put it more accurately, to provide the cushion against the deflationary forces exerted on the currency due to engaging in trade based on the Gold Standard. Thus, the Scramble for Africa by the European powers during the latter part of the nineteenth century and the first decade of the twentieth century was an alternative, but by no means a complete rescue effort on the part of the state by engaging beyond the laissez-faire doctrine. To understand the obsession with laissez-faire economics back then among the men of influence, think of today's liberal elite's love for a borderless world, or what is in most circles called "globalization" – treated as though it somehow is a law of nature.

Since the national labor market (primarily an element of the Self-regulating market) and the International Gold Standard, having enacted, together posed a more significant threat on the economic front especially after the Age of Industrial revolution commenced and also the shortage of raw materials on the European continent became a phenomenon. Thus the Scramble for Africa may be seen as a one giant step in the long sweeping protective measures enacted over the preceding century within that system.

As the Scramble for Africa began, Germany, Austria-Hungary, and Italy formed the Triple Alliance agreement in 1882, assuring mutual support in the event of an attack by any other power.

Entente Cordiale, the Anglo-French agreement in 1904, having settled the matters over Morocco and Egypt ended antagonism between Britain and France, whereby Britain and

France each clearing the way for control of Egypt and Morocco respectively. The Anglo-Russian Entente, the pact between Britain and Russia in 1907, settled the colonial disputes in Persia and Afghanistan. After Germany allowed the treaty with Russia to lapse in 1890, France and Russia made a secret alliance, completing their talks with Dual Alliance in 1894, each seeking the other's support in the event of war against Germany for France, and against Austria-Hungary for Russia. Thus with the Anglo-Russian agreement, the Triple Entente association between Britain, France, and Russia led to the emergence of the Allied Powers in the Great War.

The delicate act of the Balance of Power system – the act of restoring balance by three or more weaker units uniting against the aggressive unit – came to an end when the Concert of Europe – the loose federation of independent powers, the four entente powers of Europe, Great Britain, France, Germany, and Russia – were replaced by the two hostile power groups, the Triple Alliance and the Triple Entente. The inevitable fallout from the International Gold Standard as the Entente powers rejected trade outside their colonies and friendly states, and the aggression among them, leading to such crises as the two Moroccan crises in the Scramble, thereby effectively ended the Balance of Power system and the breakdown of the Concert of Europe. That had paved the way for war to absolutely resolve the question of dominance in the Colonial enterprise. Thus the Great War was the fight for colonies acquired prior to the eventual fallout.

Liberal Statesmen in Paris

At the end of the Great War, the then US president Woodrow Wilson – a political scientist and president of Princeton University before he became the 28th US President – along with the Prime Minister of France Georges Clemenceau, the Prime Minister of the United Kingdom David Lloyd George, and the Prime Minister of Italy Vittorio Emanuele Orlando, had together made all major decisions at the 1919 Paris Peace Conference that had led to the drafting of the Treaty of Versailles. The Treaty squarely laid the blame on aggression of Germany and her allies and paved the way for expensive reparations that could never have been paid in full and megalomaniacal territorial adjustments that could never have seemed to work for peaceful ends. And thus, by doing so, the treaty broke away from the Armistice agreed between the victors and the losers of the War based on Wilson's fourteen points, humiliating Germany in the process and the outcome of peace negotiations.

Just until a year before the Peace Conference opened the doors, Imperial Germany had proven herself the most powerful nation in Europe, having defeated Russia, Romania, Italy and having fought Britain and France to a draw for four years until the United States entered the War on the side of Allies, all the while without having one foreign soldier set foot on the German soil. After the Versailles, millions of Germans immediately found themselves living under the rule of Danes, Belgians, Italians, Poles and soon Lithuanians. Habsburg Empire received no less a treatment as the empire was dissolved, its land stripped, and people of different ethnicities scattered in the new and old territories.

The contrast between Germany's incomplete defeat at the time of the surrender that in and itself turned out to be very unpopular within the army, and particular sections of German people, and even as the onerous burden laid on the German nation in the Treaty of Versailles began to affect the people who had turned bitter and bent on revenge after losing the War. The uncanny situation that Germany found herself in – on one side having fought the War to success only to see it slip away at the last hour, and on other hand after agreeing to Armistice that paved the way for massive reparations and German border adjustments – fueled the rage among the people, who later vociferously channeled their support for such dissenting groups during the 1920s. The progressive liberal Woodrow Wilson's disregard in the Treaty of Versailles for national sentiment, the historical context within which the country came together, the deep expression of the people in the vibrant and coherent forces for the creation and sustainment of that German nation-state, and in addition the effects from the Self-regulating and decision to rejoin the International Gold Standard marked a slew of new wrong turns bringing misery to the entire European continent throughout the 1920s, the 1930s and beyond.

Tumultuous History of Germany: the Memories of a Nation

Notwithstanding the fact that the territory such as Alsace and Lorraine that previously belonged to the German nation had long remained in contentious state, in the Age of Nation-state, the stripping away of German lands and the scattering of German people had set forth the statesmen-induced counterforce against the forces for the preservation and the sustainment of German nation. Thus the seeds for the next major War had been sown at the Paris Peace Conference in the form of Treaty of Versailles, whose architects were clueless about their decisions and the consequences their actions entailed.

What should be of interest at this point is the history behind the making of the German nation, or more specifically the history of the multiple barriers that kept the realization of the German nation a distant dream. In the entire Western Civilization, the story of realization of the German nation-state at the turn of twentieth-century has been circumstantially different, as is the same with any other country, but in the case of Germany the past disasters had played into its realization and to its sustainment more profoundly than anyone, at least on the European continent from the perspective of other Western countries.

Among the cluster of kingdoms and princely states that comprised the Holy Roman Empire since the beginning of second millennia to first decade of nineteenth-century, there existed only a tenuous relationship. But territorial adjustments, resulting mostly after fighting wars, were perennial phenomena. In the sixteenth century, Martin Luther's Reformation shook up the Christian faith that characterized the European continent for a thousand years up to that point. The battle of religions from the early sixteenth to the mid-seventeenth century was supposedly based on religious acrimony but was partly an excuse to satiate the thirst for territorial expansion for most of the Western kingdoms, including those resided within the Holy Roman Empire. The religious wars between Catholics, Protestants, and Calvinists started with a lot of zeal but ended with deadly consequences. The most brutal of the confrontations among the then powers of Europe was the Thirty-years War (1618 – 1648).

The seemingly innocuous confrontation – known as the Bohemian rebellion in which the Bohemian estates staged an uprising against the ruling dynasty of Habsburgs – escalated into a widespread and full-scale European War that forced Kings and Emperors into ignoring even the supposed barriers to conflict escalation such as relationships of kinship that existed among the princes on the European continent.

The Germanic people, habituated between the French kingdom to the East, Poland to the West, the Baltic Sea and Pomerania (until 1815 when the full province became part of Prussia) to the North, the Swiss Alps and the Italian peninsula to the South, bore the brunt of War because most of the battles had been fought on Germanic lands. In this course, the Thirty-years War destroyed the kingdoms of the Holy Roman Empire, including the kingdom of Prussia, then a relatively small princely state based in Brandenburg that by some stroke of luck and effort was able to recoup and recover in over a century after the war.

The Germanic people have been killed, their homes, their villages ravaged, plundered and decimated during the War in ways that horrifies the mind. Cultural thread was torn apart; family lore that endures in the generational families became extinct; memories passed from one generation to the next shattered. About one-fourth to one-third of German people died. Many of the ones who escaped death had succumbed to starvation and disease, leading to some reports of cannibalism. With the state having disappeared their life hung between panic and instant death; their property pillaged and ravaged; a settlement of people that once exhibited the little joys of civilization turned into an abject place of desolation and destitution.

The miseries caused by the Thirty-years War had ingrained in the psyche, actively manifesting in real-time over ensuing decades and centuries in the divisions of many kingdoms and of German people, and in the perceptible threat of the increasingly mighty neighboring conquerors such as the fully-united French Empire to the West and the South, the Austro-Hungarian Empire and the Russian Empire to the East. The struggle to unify the German people under one banner drove the course of events, especially after the threat posed by Napoleon evaporated, and importantly to avoid the fateful events of shame brought up repeatedly on the German people of Prussia.

When the Napoleon army marched victoriously into the Prussian heartland in 1806 after it suffered a humiliating defeat at Jena and Auerstedt that caused King Fredrick William III and

Luise of Prussia to flee eastwards, the fate of the Kingdom of Prussia hung in balance. Under pressure from Tsar Alexander, Napoleon had agreed to keep the state of Prussia, but only after having it stripped down to its bare bones. The Kingdom had to cede its past territorial acquisitions – the Polish Provinces, and Western territories that were then annexed by France. The King sent his wife Luise to beg the Emperor for a more generous settlement – an incidental occurrence that evoked parallels with the 1630s when the then King George William desultorily sent the women-folk in Berlin to negotiate with the approaching Swedish King Gustavus Adolphus. The Treaty of Tilsit (1807) mollified Prussian ambitions; the vision of Prussia as a great eastern power dealing on an equal footing with Russia and Austria vanished.

In the aftermath, it took a remarkable turnaround of life and politics in Prussia and the will to proceed with the reacquisition and the eventual unification of Germany in the sixty to seventy years after that. And it became possible only by defeating the neighboring kingdoms, first, the Austro-Hungarian Empire (1866) and then the French Empire (1871). Thus the German people, even as many millions had continued to live outside it, had united under one nation and the rule of Prussian Prince Wilhelm I, crowned the German Emperor in the Hall of Mirrors at the Versailles Palace.

It was ironic that the Versailles Palace that came to symbolize the founding and the unification of the German nation-state and the German people (1871) would about fifty years later host the conference that drafted the Treaty of Versailles ordering the ceding of the control of a portion of national territory. As the struggles and horrors of history that were richly plastered all through the heart-and-soul of the creature called Germany, alarmingly the repetition of disintegration of the people and this time of the nation had seemed to reoccur.

A point of significant value to be noted at this juncture is that when we look upon history, we unwittingly tend to see the course of events from the present to the past and tie them together with an armchair comfort in the absolute knowledge that all of these events have transpired as they had; but all too often we forget that for the people living at the time, it was never an assurance but rather of uncertainty in which way what course of events would transpire and what may be the characteristic features of them.

For example, when Germany invaded France during the Second World War, the news sent shockwaves throughout the world because nobody believed it could be executed, or at the least, doubted there might be of any real value to it even if it could be done. We know ever since that Germany did invade France, which we take it for granted as if such an event was given, or bound to have happened, without realizing that hardly anyone ever expected it before it occurred. After all, the French military superseded that of the German.

The thirst for revenge and the unmitigated desire for retaking the lost-territory and proceeding with unification, amidst the demonstrable failures of the democratic process, had lent credence to mass politics and led among other factors including the shortcomings of the Self-regulating market to the rise of Fascism.

The Unrelenting Desire for Conquest and Colony

The process of unification of Germany, Italy, and Japan under one polity had culminated roughly at the same time, occurring just after the dawn of the Age of Industrial revolution.

Even though the colonial enterprise dream for these new nation-states at the turn of twentieth-century may have been stoked by an urgent need for a cushion to counter the negative forces of the International Gold Standard, it had not gone unnoticed that the European entente powers Great Britain, France, and Russia have had accumulated sizable colonies and territories. Thus the case for colonies after the Age of Colonial Expansion had ended came around the need for land and resources, as may be deduced from the writings of the masters who launched the Late Age of Colonial Expansion.

Germany, along with the US, and to a lesser extent Great Britain and France, was the standard bearer of the Industrial Revolution, unlike Japan, which was and is not a part of Western civilization.

Even though unification of Germany and Japan occurred at the same time, economic development of Japan lagged that of Germany. Industrialization in Germany had practically characterized the Age of Industrial Revolution. But industrialization in Japan had to wait until the Eastern nation had become Western enough, which they had in a compressed timeline (1880 – 1925), in the technical education, to accumulate and assimilate the technology of Heavy Industry that was developed in the Western countries. It may be regarded that the Japanese conquests and aggression in the Korean peninsula, events before the beginning of the Great War, were similar to the early conquests of pre-Industrial but semi-modern Great Britain and France during sixteenth, seventeenth, and eighteenth centuries.

It was when the Japanese had begun their industrialization in the mid-1920s and started to behave aggressively for foreign land that set off the alarm bells among the Allied powers. Like Germany, Japan had become concerned about population, land, and later about major industrial resources such as oil. Japan recorded a population spike during the 1920s, 1930s and scarcity of land therefore had turned out to be a major issue.

With major powers bordering all sides capable of doing lasting damage in the depths of the Thirty-years War, the mission for Germany to reclaim territory slipped from pre-War Germany was nevertheless the implicit sub-factor in the ultimate factors that led to another War. Fear of the neighboring powers, whose actions encapsulated in the German division that lay long before the unification, the unfavorable outcome from the Peace Conference, and the thirst for more land during the 1930s on the part of Third Reich underscores the role played by Geography.

Moreover, in the case of Japan too, Geography rules. Firstly, the isolation of the Japanese island had itself set off and contributed, at the least, in part, to the entirely different route the country had taken from the Asian counterparts. Secondly, the uneven balance between the scarce livable land and the growing population during the times of industrial upheaval had been a major cause for concern to the rulers.

Additionally, in the face of growing land and resource problems, the dramatic effects of the deflationary spirals from the International Gold Standard intensified as the country accumulated Heavy Industry capital; and power was captured by the military from the ineffective civilian rulers in the face of daunting forces of instability. The International Gold Standard had spiraled out and spread the deflationary forces to other industrial trading countries. And it may be just that resulting economic crisis seemed to be the necessary break to turn around popular support from the ineffective to the supposedly effective, whether it was a party or an armed force, as has been the case in Germany and Japan. The German and Japanese constitutions that allowed the dictators and the militants to seize power did not differ much in the content since Japan had copied the German constitution previously.

Italian Fascism in the US and in other allied countries lost popular appeal as soon as Mussolini, in the spirit of Hitler's lead, invaded Abyssinia (now Ethiopia) in 1935. But it was only as the horrors of the Holocaust became evident that Italian Fascism, which bent to Hitler's demand to round up the Jews in the Northern and central Italy, became permanently tainted (more on this later).

Thus in the Age that followed the Age of Colonial Expansion, Germany and Italy once again, and Japan together re-launched what we have termed the Late Age of Colonial Expansion, kindling the forces of collision with the Axis powers and thus with War itself.

Since the time the Fascist and Militarist regimes consolidated power in those countries during the 1930s, the thirst for colonies intensified as they had sought to solve the problems plaguing them. With Germany additionally having to recuperate displaced territory, the aggression and the vent for revenge carried to its natural state – killing, attacking and conquering any group, be it a party, race, or a nation, identified as the enemy, culminating in yet another disastrous war, the Second World War.

Chapter Five

Liberalism Unfolding in Twentieth Century

The Course Correction

Europe took center stage in the drama of the fallout from nineteenth century Liberalism. However it has been in the United States where the drama of liberalization of society, closely followed but sometimes surpassed in the extent by the European countries, had unfolded during the twentieth century. After the Great War, the US took the seat of the headquarters of world finance from Great Britain and after the Second World War the position of supreme power in the free nations.

In the United States, the social impact from the deflationary effects of the laissez-faire economy and the International Gold Standard had come to a head. Especially the devastating crisis sparked following the 1906 San Francisco earthquake had sent the dollar into deflationary mode for the next two years (see Fig. 4.1). The United States, the industrial country that was outside the balance of powers of Europe, had begun to transform laissez-faire-economics-guided state (– 1913) to interventionist state.

Therefore at the turn of the twentieth century, as the US couldn't hold back any more of the unforeseen effects from having the Self-regulated market and the International Gold Standard, the time for course correction to the doctrine and therefore to the role of the state in the affairs of the economy had duly arrived. Because the course of events turned out to reveal the flaw in its recommendation of laissez-faire state, Liberalism corrected the doctrine, in the mold of sound doctrine rectifying and keeping up with the real world. Thus, the doctrine of Liberalism in the early twentieth century reversed its course from the ideal of laissez-faire-economics-guided state to an interventionist state.

Therefore in the United States, during the first and the second decade of twentieth century, as the Age of Industrial Revolution ended, and the Age of Modernization began, the state was transformed from one of laissez-faire to interventionist by way of enacting Constitutional amendments wherever necessary, and by way of legislating institutions to intervene in the matters of economy.

Thus far, the doctrine of Liberalism turned around the state in the eighteenth century from the cruel, oppressive and tyrannical to liberal, and in the nineteenth century liberalized economy from the grips of state, or stopped the state from taking control by way of its swaying advocacy for laissez-faire economics on the part of the state. But in the matters of the economy at the turn of the twentieth century in the US and after the end of the turmoil in Europe, the laissez-faire state had been given way to the interventionist state.

Having turned the state and the economy into liberal and having corrected the prior prescription, later on, the doctrine of Liberalism, like the good doctrine trying to keep being relevant, embarked on a new mission in the twentieth century; but this time on a mission to liberalizing society.

How did this course correction arrive? What was the driving force operating underneath the tectonic shifts that in addition to resulting in a reverse turn in the relationship between market and state also carried monumental changes in regards to the relationship between individual and state? That phenomenon traces its roots to what may be called the Great Awakening, and to which we'll turn next.

The Great Awakening

Across the Western world since the latter half of the nineteenth century, an intellectual awakening swept the halls of Academia. That awakening has its footing in the unexpected provision of new evidence to revive the ideas of eighteenth century enlightenment. That awakening essentially rejuvenated Liberalism's religion and tradition dimension, and modified the economic dimension, and gave full intellectual thrust to that quasi-religious ideology that is Liberalism that has been influencing the course of events to this day. The intellectuals of that time attuned to the glorious developments that ushered the awakening had endeavored to make the most out of them.

The socio-political state of the French Revolution, about which we'll explore later on, quickly receded, never to come back as the Ancién Regime was somewhat restored. Therefore the dream of the revolutionaries to create and sustain a new atheistic state religion – in the line of respecting and worshipping reason – had faded. But the intellectual energy of the French Enlightenment of the eighteenth century did not go away as it carried on into the nineteenth century in different modes of thoughts and movements, and the one that most famously claims a direct lineage to the late nineteenth century Great Awakening was the movement or the ideology called Positivism. The philosophy of Positivism was mostly a repackaging of the enlightenment ideas of reason and logic, the importance of sensual experience and data, etc. But the movement besides this fundamental affirmation also advocated for an outright repudiation of metaphysics and any such transcendent knowledge lacking evidence (such as the existence of God). Positivism, as formulated and evolved from the theories of the movement's most visible figure Auguste Comte (1798 – 1857), was secular and anti-metaphysical in the posture.

The storm that ushered in the Great Awakening may be divided into these three familiar dimensions– economic, religion, and tradition, to draw in an intimate and precise account. But the full stock of ideas underpinning the Awakening was together transformative and revolutionary in that it ushered in a new outlook on the whole phenomena of life on the planet earth.

In the spirit and the awe of the then intellectual revolution shining a different light on human origins, morals, and history, the moment when Man could finally be set free from the oppressive institutions of religion and the cumbersome codes of tradition had arrived. Additionally, the hour of history when the proletariat masses revolt against the capitalist masters to set free from the chains of systemic exploitation had also come – as encapsulated in the Marxist prophesy of the proletariat revolution being on the horizon.

With rich lineage tracing to Thomas Moore's *Utopia* (1516), the dreams of organizing a more evolved, more modern society seemed to come true. As a matter of a great deal, the idea of society evolving to a more modern form seemed to be manifestly correct as the fruits of Industrial revolution since the mid-1870s that began the modernization of the traditional economic activities and along with it the lifestyle as well vividly suggested. Modern machines, modern goods, modern philosophy (on social organization) seemed to imply that the society was progressing and indeed in the process of ascendance to a modern form.

The method of analyzing in the three-dimensional structure of the phenomena-at-hand may not strictly comport with the actual inter-linkages, multi-framework influences characteristic of the time, as was of the enlightenment; but with some generalization, we may proceed. The figures who spearheaded that storm were Karl Marx on the economic dimension, Charles Darwin on the religious dimension and Friedrich Nietzsche on the tradition dimension. On the economic front, building on the ideas of the British socialists such as Robert Owen, Karl Marx began to wage vigorous attacks on the then existing Capitalist economic system of production and distribution. Marx came up with a pseudo-scientific theory called historical materialism – a way of looking at history and the transformative cycles within it – from which he deduced that the time for proletariat revolution was on the horizon.

On the religion front, Charles Darwin's theory of evolution by natural selection opened the door more thoroughly than ever before for the consideration of quixotic approaches – or specifically, political movements local to the country – in the line of reason replacing that of traditional religion. But at that time it wasn't quite clear how this development in practice would unfold. In the previous century the French Enlightenment thinkers most famously Voltaire had already concluded that the Bible was a sham; the French revolutionaries in practice took this to logical conclusion and tried to enact a new state religion – one that worshipped reason.

During the late nineteenth century, however, it didn't matter what would come next. Because of the new light on the human origins and the whole evolutionary process of competition inherent to the idea of survival of the fittest, the case for radical social engineering at least seemed to exit. Because of explosive population being a standard feature in those decades, the idea of social engineering yielded one another concept that had proved uniformly relevant to all of the movements that came out of this upheaval: Darwinian eugenics. At any length, the answer to the question of what fills the vacuum in the absence of religious authority, or after having ensured the lack of it, came from the newly emerging economic front itself and it was none other statism – the worship of the state. Karl Marx's socialist theories dripped with tendencies culminating in the state control not only of the economic system but everything.

On the tradition front, Fredric Nietzsche launched the first full-frontal assault on the Judeo-Christian values of the West, or more specifically, the basis of those values. Nietzsche was preoccupied with the origins and function of values in human life – that is the role of the rights and wrongs, good and bad in the affairs of life and the creation of them in the first place. Naturally, this meant for Nietzsche to probe the motives behind the values that defined the West. In this quest, he had come to characterize the full stock of Western philosophy, religion, and morality as an ascetic ideal.

First Nietzsche deduced a theory of master morality and slave morality; he argued that while master morality was concerned with good and bad, the distinction was only descriptive because it was about the privileged masters alone as opposed to the slaves. In contrast, slave morality supposed the good versus evil distinction, and this arose, he wrote, when the slaves avenged themselves by converting the attributes of mastery into vices. Additionally, Nietzsche reckoned that slave morality's claim to be the only true morality was the essential aspect of its survival. It was this insistence on absoluteness, he wrote, that turned out to be the principal feature of the making of religious ethics.

With the collapse of the metaphysical and theological foundations and sanctions for traditional morality, he concluded, only a pervasive sense of meaninglessness and purposelessness would emerge – meaning the triumph of nihilism. Thus Nietzsche opened the door by his critique of traditional morality or more specifically the origins of it. He declared, "God is dead."

Marxism, Communism, Fascism, Progressivism, Liberalism

On the three fronts, the nature and the kind of impact the philosophies and ideas of those three figures differed widely. On this note, it may help to distinguish the transformative wave in various spheres of effects: attack, alternative, and tactics. The ideas of all the three constituted an attack on the institutions within the respective fronts, but only Marx proposed an alternative way forward. In practice, even the alternative coming from the economic front also filled the void on the religion front, as noted already. This gigantic wave of sweeping societal change on the European continent culminated into what we have come to call Marxian Socialism, and on the United States as Progressivism. It was from these two original movements that the derivative siblings and cousins saw the light of the day, including Fascism, Socialism, Communism, Nazism, Fabian Socialism, Modern Liberalism, Leninism, Technocracy, Corporatism, and War Socialism. These movements have acclimatized with the location but shared the same intellectual wellspring.

The flavor local to the United States had been renamed to Liberalism (Modern Liberalism) and only, later on, came to be called thus. With renewed social and economic aims that underlay these movements, the general principle that underscored all of them was that the state should be allowed to get away with anything, so long as it was for "good reasons." That was viewed as the triumph of pragmatism in politics, sweeping away any formal boundaries to the scope of state power.

Rich in anti-religion and anti-tradition front, and with the newly fixed pro-state intervention of the economy on the economic dimension, this rejuvenated and reversed-on-the-economic-front doctrine of Liberalism had, therefore, emerged from the new intellectual thrust fired up by the theories of Darwin, Nietzsche, and Marx. The sister movements under different banners and labels matured to national significance across the West. And likewise Liberalism ascended into the collective conscience in the United States.

Classical Liberalism – that version of Liberalism with an emphasis on the political and economic dimension – had paved way to Modern Liberalism – that version of Liberalism with an emphasis on the social dimension (religion and tradition) and reversed-economic dimension, thus the transition from Classical Liberalism's Individualism to Modern Liberalism's Collectivism.

Further, these movements had found in the idea of the "general will" an intellectual tool to supplant the then realigned view of the relationship between the individual and society, wherein individuals could not be free, except as part of the group or the collective. In this tradition, Leninism, Fascism, Technocracy, Fabian Socialism, Corporatism, War Socialism, German Social Democracy were all applied Marxism or Socialism, which had flirted with the intellectual men across the West and enthralled the society with its mesmerizing spirit of "collectivism." The major difference in the application of the doctrine of Marxism or Socialism not only split the intellectuals but also gave rise to local flavors within the international underpinnings of the original movement, reflected in slogans like "the workers of the world unite." But everywhere in practice, it culminated into an all-caring, all-encompassing, all-powerful state that had come to replace God. Statism reigned supreme in all of these doctrines. The worship of government became the new thing; it's because the government then came to be seen as the ideal and useful tool to solve everything and reorganize the society in a more modern form.

As for the tactics to execute the movements in practice, to usher in the change these doctrines intended to bring, the direction to this effect came from Marx himself. Marx prophesied that the workers would rise against the capitalist masters and expropriate the means of production. But to the socialists awaiting the proletarian revolution, the uprising had never arrived. It looked as though Marx prophesy had failed. That's where the ideas of Italian Marxist Antonio Gramsci (1891 – 1937) and the French socialist George Sorel (1847 – 1922) came in and filled the void. But first, we have to uncover one major setback that struck this movement on the Continent.

The blow that struck the wellspring movement that was the Socialist International movement, widely known as the Second International (1889 – 1916) that was replaced after its collapse by the Communist International or merely the Comintern, was the betrayal of the Leftist, Communist and Socialist parties in the West. In the interests of their respective countries, those Parties all over the West except in few places had declared support, or voted for the declaration or the funding of War that was the Great War. The ensuing war was perceived as being supposedly waged by the greedy imperial Capitalists whom the international movement had bitterly resented and had advocated until then to resist their attempts to start a war. The move by these parties in the direction opposite to the advocated stance came as shocking and greatly disaffected the spirit of the movement as the Second International came to be dissolved in the midst of the War in 1916.

It is in this context and after having already waited for the revolution that never materialized that the diagnosis and the solutions of the two philosophers Gramsci and Sorel came to fore. The Marxist Gramsci diagnosed that the reason the workers failed to rise was because of the fact that religion, strong family values and loyalty to one's country held too much influence in the working-class families. Gramsci further argued that as a precursor to the revolution, the cultural hegemony of the old traditions had to be dismantled. The only way to destroy the old order, he said, was to launch a long march through the elite cultural institutions – takeover the culture, erase the old traditions including religion and remake it to be ripe for revolution. What this would amount to is a form of Culture War, and the process "Cultural Marxism."

The socialist George Sorel did not have that much patience. If Marx's prophecy of the proletariat revolution failed to realize, Sorel concluded, give it the illusion of reality for it be achieved; if only the workers realized their organizing power and declared a general strike, capitalism and the masters would be crushed to the ashes. Therefore, mobilizing the masses in that direction by the few myth creators – in the style of Lenin and Mussolini – was deemed to be the only way forward. Sorel theorized "the power of the myth" by marrying William James' notion of the "will to believe," and Nietzsche's "will to power." Mussolini who was Sorel's greatest student echoed the same later in a 1932 interview, "It is faith that moves mountains, not reason. Reason is a tool, but it can never be the motive force of the crowd."

To this notion, Sorel theorized further the role of violence to bring in the revolution. He declared that because force was the state's power of coercion, the use of violence by the revolutionary insurgents was the denial of the existing socio-political order. Ever since, the notions of "myth" and "violence" became a central theme of the revolutionary spirit carried by all of those derivative movements. Lenin, Mussolini, Hitler were deeply inspired as the idea of the myth and the use of violence were central for their respective parties to eclipse to power. But Hitler and Mussolini took Sorel's ideas to heart only after having deviated from the international socialist trend.

For Hitler and Mussolini, their brief participation in the Great War opened their eyes to the absurdity of the internationally aligned, class-based Socialist movement's attempts to overthrow Capitalism. To them it became utterly clear that men fought and sacrificed their lives for their country, for culture, for family, and not for some pseudo-class of workers.

The Marxist prophecy of proletariat revolution had not come true. For Socialism to be achieved, Mussolini wrote that it had to be transformed from the international kind of socialism to socialism in one state, and that therefore it was manifestly necessary for the old socialist party standing against this efforts to be crushed. Mussolini declared, "to assassinate the Party in order to save Socialism." Hitler himself became utterly convinced that the Internal movement was going nowhere. Besides, from the early days of his romance with Socialism, Hitler harbored doubts on the Marxist-flavored Socialism known as the International Socialist movement. That was because in his view Karl Marx belonged to the grand Jewish conspiracy. Therefore, Socialism without Marx proved a much more attractive movement.

From that point the Marx-inspired International Socialist movement had morphed into a movement of National Socialism and the Italian variety of socialism known as Fascism. These flavors of Socialism with nationalistic bent competed with the original Socialist parties. The break for these parties in Europe clamoring for power came from the inbred fury among the masses over the tired, same-old liberal democratic politics that had failed to solve any of the shakeups of the time, characteristically caused by Self-regulating market and the International Gold Standard. But disheartening shifts and changes in the aftermath of the Great War and the Great Depression crucially enabled these parties to reach the halls of power.

Additionally the Industrial revolution, just as it did to other traditional activities, revolutionized the traditional mode of communication and enabled the advent of the Age of Mass (Mob) Politics that so significantly shaped the path these movements took in their quest for power. After rising to power, the feasibility for implementing these doctrinal precepts was found only during emergencies, created advertently or inadvertently. Thus the permanent emergencies witnessed in the countries in Europe where they were being implemented. To that effect, they have exploited the semi-emergency situations to permanently destroy the old socio-political institutions in the country as quickly as possible, even as the Press was promptly run over by the Party men.

Progressivism and Liberalism in the United States

The United States did not remain immune to the forces of change being swept across the lands of Europe. As a matter of fact, the US antedated Europe in the implementation, but did so in a subtle, more stylistic fashion. Both the Democratic Party and the Republican Party had been transformed and taken into the folds of Progressive movement at the time, in addition to the Progressive Party created for the same singular purpose. Thus in 1912 all the three Presidential candidates identified themselves as progressives, and aimed to implement progressive policies – the state control of the economy – at the seat of power. In the General Election, the Republican vote split between the incumbent President William Howard Taft, and his predecessor Theodore Roosevelt guaranteed the victory of radical democrat Woodrow Wilson.

Wilson was the philosopher-president who embarked on an idea to radically remake the Presidency, and consolidate power. Wilson was awarded one of the first PhDs in political science by Johns Hopkins University. His exceptional career as a professor of political science across many institutions of higher learning propelled him to the presidency of Princeton University in 1902. He ran for governor in New Jersey in 1910, which he handily won. While in his early career Wilson, as a leading progressive voicing support for the consolidation of power at the center, picked out Congress as the best organ for that purpose. But after observing Teddy Roosevelt's success in remaking the presidency into one of the center of all power in Washington, Wilson changed his mind. He began to see the Presidency as the most effective branch to expand and consolidate power. Thus in 1912, he threw his hat into the contest for the Democratic Party ticket for president, which he won in the 46th ballot after deadlocks in earlier ballots. His presidency was an attempt at creating the utopian society.

As the United States entered the Great War on the side of Allies, the emergency conditions created out of the war turned out to be the most favorable period for the realization of the progressive agenda. Even prior to the entry the Wilson administration already had some of the most far-reaching laws legislated – the Federal Reserve Act (1913) created the powerful Fed, the Federal Trade Commission Act (1914) expanding on the Bureau of Corporations established by Roosevelt, in conjunction with the Clayton Antitrust Act (1914), to curtail unfair practices by businesses, and the Federal Farm Loan Act (1916) creating a farm loan board to oversee federal land, banks and national farm loan associations. Many of these Acts have substantially increased government control of the business and the economy. During the war, the War Industries Board was created to replace the long established but weak General Munitions Board to coordinate production and distribution. The new board set production quotas and allocated raw materials. Although the Board was decommissioned after the War, it served as the model for the Franklin Roosevelt administration, itself engaged in the Depression era emergency, to reenact permanently the same, culminating in the Alphabet-soup agencies. During the War, Wilson also oversaw the legislation of the Espionage Act of 1917 and the Sedition Act of 1918 that under the cloud of War turned to be extremely useful to suppress dissenting voices, including that of the press.

After the War, the next major break in the US to implement the ideals of Progressive movement came in the aftermath of the 1929 Stock Market Crash. The Great Depression had wholly and starkly invalidated the notions of the Self-regulating market and the International Gold Standard; the insipid and inept doctrine of economic liberalism (the laissez faire principle in the economic dimension of Classical Liberalism) had come to be seen as an utter failure and that the only path forward or the remedy to the chaotic times of the early 1930s came to reside in the chic and exotic statism in regards to the economic front – that being the state control of the economic sectors, directly, or indirectly.

As Progressive policies that characterized the Great War lost appeal and gradually faded during the Roaring Twenties, they had since the 1930s rejuvenated and taken a different name in 'Liberalism,' which had come to be identified with the label "Modern Liberalism" in the US for to be contrasted with the previous century version of European Liberalism called "Classical Liberalism." Franklin Roosevelt – who served as Secretary of Navy in the Wilson administration and admired the courageous policies being implemented during the Great War – mimicked those policies but adopted under different banner. His administration copied and enacted the models of Wilson's wartime model of state regulation and mobilization of resources, but this time on a broader scale and steeply interventionist on a permanent basis.

Thus, in the matter of few decades and just under few administrations, from 1913 to 1920 and once more in the aftermath of the Great Depression 1933 to 1935, and yet again after the entry into the Second World War 1942 to 1945, the United States, under the banner of Progressivism and

Liberalism, had been transformed to one that believes in and strives for big government, collectivism, equality and justice, thereby eschewing the ideals of Republicanism of limited government and individual freedom. In the UK, the Beveridge Report published in the middle of the Second World War recommended to the state to address the myriad social welfare problems. Hugely popular with the public, the proposals in the document formed the basis on which Great Britain charted the course in the postwar era, establishing the Welfare state, the National Health Services etc.

Liberalization of Society

If "freedom" and "liberty" were the values that animated Liberalism before the turn of twentieth century and that advocated and advanced the cause of liberalizing the state and the economy, then the new values that gripped this doctrine to its cause in the twentieth century were "equality" and "justice." However, one is prompted to ask, why only those values? As we will see, the preaching of "equality" and "justice" is the blow horn through which the doctrine effortlessly brings sections of society into liberal fold.

Modern Liberalism's anti-religious and anti-tradition front means the eradication of all things traditional, dogmatic, customary, habitual, irrational that had gripped the society since time immemorial. This essentially amplifies into what may be called the liberalization of society from dogma, faith, revelation, tradition etc. Modern Liberalism seeks to replace religion with reason, tradition with pragmatism– essentially an application of reason.

But what does liberalization of society mean? Liberal transformation of society is essentially a dramatic turnaround of the nature of relationships among people themselves in the direction of the gradual eradication of all of the traditional groups and all of the identities that come with them. This eventually is the route toward eradicating from society all things traditional and those institutions that have relationship with the past.

In retrospect, it is not all too illogical to see why Liberalism came to move away from the ideals of freedom to the ideals of equality (which includes equality of justice, and that term sometimes quietly stands alongside merely as "justice"). The doctrine promotes the ideals of "equality" and "justice" to deploy the powerful force in "state" to this effect. That is, the state is geared as the mechanism through which the transformation of society – to gradually eradicate all of the traditional groupings and identities – in the mold of liberalism is carried out. These ideals also at times take in different forms in "tolerance" or "fairness."

But in practice what does it mean to promote the ideals of "equality" and "justice" that are central to the doctrine of Liberalism making inroads along the three dimensions – economic, religion and tradition – during the twentieth century?

To start, the ideals of "equality" and "justice" of the doctrine would not have had the power of gospel if it weren't for the existence of a certain section of society genuinely deserving "equality" and "justice," an existence due to factors of historical or economic circumstance. As an example, during the twentieth century the economic under development of African Americans in the United States, in addition to the fight for civil rights and political representation, was of political and socio-economic nature. And henceforth one can logically make a case without pulling the levers of a magnificent doctrine for deserving resource deployment from the state to the people, up to a specific sphere and time, notwithstanding the consequences whether positive or negative that entail from that undertaking.

But that is not where the doctrine of Liberalism stops. Modern Liberalism, through liberals, unceasingly identifies what one may call "the people of the lower strata" of society – with labels like the poor, the vulnerable and the oppressed etc. – residing within the country, and later even abroad, whether the strata is tempered on racial, cultural, national, family, gender, or any other such type of grouping. Over time the liberal society tries to blur the difference between the traditional creations and the liberal concoctions – mainly any clusters of people more parochial than mankind to decimate the traditional creatures whether they are abstract or natural in the creation.

Liberalism through the liberals hamstrings and cripples the idea of national sovereignty, and erases the difference between citizens and foreign aliens to erode the privileges of the citizens and destroy the mechanism through which people with common identity tries to create a shared destiny; to this effect encourages multiculturalism to dilute the culture upon which the common identity rests on; advocates liberal divorce laws to weaken the spirit of marriage and loosen the bonds of matrimony; and cultivates nihilistic attitude to sex eroding the development of virtues inherent to each gender and parent that are essential to raising healthy, virtuous children.

This mechanism of operation on all of these traditional fronts has been paramount toward advancing the cause of the liberalization of society – essentially the phenomena amounting to Culture Wars, and the mechanism being Gramsci's Cultural Marxism. The long march through the institutions was a success, as was the ability to wage wars to destroy the old traditions including religion and the influence it exercised.

Liberal Takeover

Modern Liberalism is an ideology, just as Classical Liberalism, with its own cache of prioritized values. To believe in modern liberalism is to prioritize the values of "equality" and "justice" (or its derivative varieties). To a liberal ideologue– an ideologue in general is one whose beliefs and priorities are shuttered from refutation by logical thinking, these values sit at the top and they have to be the predominant ideals upon which the reorganization of society must happen. Modern Liberalism works through the liberals – and the takeover of the individual into this fold may be referred to as the liberal takeover of the individual, and over time, of the society at-large.

Over the course of the twentieth century, during the Age of Modernization and the Age of Speculation that followed it, the takeover of society into the fold of Modern Liberalism happened in two steps. First, and this is the one that came early on, has been the liberal takeover of the intellectual. Second, that followed the first, has been the liberal takeover of an increasingly greater share of each new generation of society. What were the causes that enabled those two takeovers?

First and foremost, the liberal takeover of the intellectual had been greatly accelerated with the incoming interventionist state. In the Age of Interventionist State (1914 –), the rise of liberal intellectual paralleled the growth of urban cities, the urban population and the urban lifestyle – a development itself due to the modernization of all activities, traditional, hence the Age of Modernization. In the Age of post-Darwin that paralleled the Age of Modernization, Liberal ideals' preaching of the care for people of lower strata of society – the poor, the vulnerable and the oppressed etc. within the country – and even abroad as identity with the country, later on, recedes as it shall in the Age of Supranational Polity, the creed of Liberalism – the fundamental beliefs, that is – of "equality" and "justice" duly replaced the religious dogma amongst the intellectuals.

The religious impulse – the quest for meaning that transcends the rational world of cause and effect – is imbued into the human spirit. That is why faith, coupled with its endurance congruent with the design and survival of societies across oceans and mountains, through the myriad civilizations from east to west, gives it the predominant role in the affairs of man, and hence its just place as the necessary dimension or feature of human civilization. The congenital human guilt, which previously faith had comforted, soothed, and provided an outlet for, imperceptibly longs for an overarching belief in something that is larger-than-individual– something in the vein of the ideals of "equality" and "justice" which rightfully are the source of Modern Liberalism's fame and popularity.

The liberal guilt – the term referring to the guilt of the liberals – is indeed a false equivalency in that the longing for an outlet for the imperceptible and everlasting guilt and the belief in the larger-than-individual ideals of Liberalism do not actually comport at all. That is, the guilt of the liberal is never soothed. Instead, the liberal outlet is one of many, if there are many more, to which the energy seeking an outlet has met the demand. Notwithstanding that, the liberal creed of the ideal of "equality" and "justice" is the foundation on which the doctrine's fame fundamentally rests, as noted above, and even as the creed finds concrete expression in such other phrases as "human rights."

Indeed the declaration of Human Rights after the Second World War was but a concrete affirmation of the Liberal creed that in due course had come to grip large sections of society, replacing the ideals of religion with the ideals of liberal creed. The expression "human rights" stands alone stripped of the source, the social context, and the larger meaning. Liberalism replaced the vacuum caused by the absence of almighty, which is the source of rights, or in the modern terms, human rights, that the American founding fathers agreed in the Declaration of Independence.

In the post-Darwin Age, the liberal transformation of intellectuals first meant the institutional takeover of the cultural megaphones by them has been necessary not only because of the ease it affords to bringing in the rest of the society, ripe for transformation in the Age of Modernization, into liberal fold, but also of the need to check the forces of anti-liberal ideas that inevitably arise over and over in time, especially as the non-liberals point out the egregiousness of the trendy liberal instincts policies.

The liberal takeover of the society has been eased by the prior existence of the moral vacuum in the people, in the Age of post-Darwin and the Age of Modernization. Free from the effects of parenting, the hollow ground has continued to provide for liberal transformation of people by means of institutional preaching – a mind that is ripe for indoctrination shall be indoctrinated. In practice, the trend clearly pointed toward an ever-decreasing share of the people of faith and an ever-rising percentage of the people subscribing to liberal creed.

Modern Liberalism taking a stronghold position in the course of unraveling in the polity and society over the twentieth century throughout the West may not only have caused but also encouraged the gradual dissolution of the Western civilization – be it in the geographic reach, economic interest, cultural mores, and importantly, national identity, and the nations.

The receding of Western civilization comprises two variations of different content: the receding and the ending of the Western domination over a non-Western society, and the end of Western hegemony within a society and region that have historically been an integral part of Western civilization.

The Decline of Western dominance in the non-Western Domain

Western Civilization had reached its peak just before the breakout of the Great War in 1914. Since then, the steady receding of the West had been visible in many different realms. The first shot to Western retreat came with the loss of Russia to Communism between 1917 and 1921. Determined to go its own way, in stark contrast to what the West had stood for, Russia took up the entire Eastern Europe into its sphere of influence in the aftermath of Second World War. The Iron curtain not only acted as the division between West and East but also symbolized a profound loss to the West.

In the postwar era, Western retreat soon precipitated. The values of "equality" and "justice" had to prevail across the world. The subjugation of the Eastern people by the oppressive Western man had to be ended. Justice to the colonized people had to be served; the bonds of equality had to be strengthened by allowing the colonies to self-determine their future.

The loss of colonies in Africa, South Asia, South East Asia and the Pacific, the physical capital accumulated, the ports and bridges, the bays and the islands, all account to an extraordinary loss to the West. Perhaps in the aggregate, the loss of wealth constitute in the order of one to one-and-a-half times the annual national income of the entire West just before the beginning of Second World War. Without the consideration of the merits or demerits of the development that was decolonization, the loss in and of itself was significant to the West. The question that has to be probed is not whether that development known as decolonization should have happened– the answer to that question has been an uncontested and clear yes, but how it happened and why only when it did.

In *Suicide of the West* (1964), James Burnham (1905 – 1987) amply showed that that what Americans call "Liberalism" had come to be the typical verbal systematization of the process of Western contraction and withdrawal, that Liberalism motivates and justifies the contraction, and reconciles the people to it.

Liberalism, Burnham noted, by a wondrous alchemy transmutes the dark defeats, withdrawals and catastrophes into their bright opposites: into gains, victories, and advances. Thus, the geographic, political, demographic and strategic losses emerge as triumphs of freedom, equality, progress and virtue.

James Burnham concludes, "Primarily, however, the ideology of modern liberalism must be understood as itself one of the expressions of the Western contraction and decline; a kind of epiphenomenon or haze accompanying the march of history; a swan song, a spiritual solace of the same order as the murmuring of a mother to a child who is gravely ill."

While the Western control over a non-Western society effectively ended, the receding of the Western domination within a society and region that has historically been an integral part of Western civilization is ongoing. The dissection of the Western retreat into the two variations, the west and the non-west, is not so much a matter of an arithmetic composition but one of systematic culmination. The Western retreat in the western domain is as much a part of the Western retreat in the non-Western domain, and vice-versa. The two variations are not so much a result in the gross distinctions in the form but one of parallel and unbroken phenomena. That is, if one variation could happen, the other inevitably would follow it or accompany it. Civilizations are not numbers that can be added, or subtracted, or divided; they thrive and they leave. The slipping of the will to survive is as much reflected in the loss of control over an extra-territorial sphere as it does within. In short, the two cannot be dissected; the distinction into the two variations is just a presentation necessity.

The Age of Consolidation of Liberalism

Liberal disdain for traditional groupings of people means their longing for swift eradication of the same, be it in terms of nation, race, religion, marriage, or gender. Should a sizable portion of liberal society emerge, and the right political landscape present itself, the liberal ideals shall be duly carried out.

The early seeds for the Age of Supranational Polity were sown in the aftermath of Second World War, as can be seen from the creation of the many multi-national entities to maintain peace, stability, to promote and enable financial co-operation and exchange, trade agreements etc. Given that the liberal disdain for Nation-state – the traditional creature that manifests itself everyday in conducting the state business and the national symbols and sermons that include the flag and the national anthem – meant that there is a strong ilk, duly presented the chance such as that one, of the liberal to see national identity swiftly receded and promptly eroded.

From our examination in Chapter three, the Age of Supranational Polity cut the cord from and succeeded the Age of Nation-state precisely when the Age of Modernization ended (and then the Age of Speculation came to the fore following it). That is why the Age of Speculation is so strongly enacted and backed by the Liberal elite and followed in the lockstep by the liberal society. And that is why *The Economist*, which preaches Globalization and Human Rights to the heartfelt of its editors, is a favorite of the liberal elite– its prime readership.

Across the West the institutions of the Media, Academia and the Arts, the three megaphones in shaping the culture and the society, as it is well known and is there for all to see day-in and day-out, is liberal. The long march in the transformation of these three vital cultural institutions into liberal fold had been underway just about since the time "the liberal intellectual" became a thing, and the process had been greatly benefited, directly and indirectly, from the fruits of the Age of Modernization (mass education programs) and the Age of the interventionist state (vast bureaucracy)– causing to remind that late-development called "Common Core" in the US was nothing but an intermingling of those two. The liberals staffing the Academia with a provision of liberal curriculum and liberal teaching in general produces the liberals who then shape the Media and the Arts. A drip of Liberalism down the books, down the classrooms, down the minds of the young students fully acclimatizes them with a world that is thoroughly infested with gross injustices as portrayed to them by the liberal teachers. The roots planted in the classrooms then materials into liberal public, the liberal voters, and the liberal media.

The interventionist state in the economic sphere, whose affairs have been modeled following the failures of the laissez-faire-economics-guided state, had to be transformed into a different mode and for a different purpose in its functioning in the Age that succeeded the Age of Modernization, thus reshaping into what may be called the "protectionist state." This transformation of state function as it comes to the regulation of economy over the past two-hundred-and-fifty years – from laissez-faire to interventionist to protectionist – has been a result of reactionary forces stimulated against other larger forces (that is, the Age of Modernization ending) rather than of an implementation of prudent academic discovery of a specific policy.

The Age of Speculation, Expansion, and Inversion could not have come about without a re-orientation of the intervening state. That what has been commonly referred to as the "Neoliberal order," it is nothing but a reoriented state serving the interests in the line of speculation, expansion, inversion in the economy. In this Age, the vast regulation of business and increased business compliance, enabled by co-opting federal bureaucracy, in the United States and Europe, the deregulation of specific activities within the financial system, the removal of trade barriers around the World, the unprecedented freedom for movement of capital and to relocate manufacturing abroad, together serve adjust and support this development in the business of Speculation, Expansion, and Inversion. Capital that take the form of investment funds cannot be associated with any nation when it has to be moved quickly with the click of a button from one country to another. A capital that is tied to a country cannot be geared for activities such as those this Age solidified.

In addition, the costly compliance and regulatory burdens, and other anti-business factors are a manifestation of policies of the protectionist state, keeping in place various mechanisms by which established businesses avoid price competition, erect monopoly protection, enact stringent barriers to easy new business entry for others, suppress and kill the rise of small businesses, state-insure the downfall and protect the upside – to the most extent an upgrade of the business-bureaucracy relation that existed prior since the time the federal bureaucracy began to intervene in the economy. In other words, the beneficiaries of the protectionist state benefited from the structure inherited from the interventionist state.

The uncontested agreement among the contemporary authors on the reappearance of Market Fundamentalism in the mold of classical economic theory (the economic front to Classical Liberalism) that supposedly characterized the neoliberal world is utterly deceiving. It actually was a selective push for, and the enforcement of specific old-school economic theories in the mode of free trade and free capital movements that benefited the businesses emerging big from the Age of Modernization. One can only see for evidence the myriad complexities in the entry of a new business, the sustainment of a small business, the expansion of a small business, and challenging a monopoly competitor.

The emergence of support for free capital movement does not mean the domestic affairs of business operations became liberalized from the stronghold of the state. Evidence of the rise of Market Fundamentalism in the Global South again can also be interpreted as the clearing out or the removal of barriers to make way for the Age of Speculation, Expansion, and Inversion. The liberalization of the Indian economy is one such example. India's reliance on foreign trade since 1991 and especially after the turn of the millennium not only benefited the Indian people and lifted millions out of poverty, as it technically should because after all the state roadblocks to doing business and trade prior to this development were too many that just dampened growth, but the corporations in the West as well. One can see for evidence in the trade data and also from a casual experience with the supporting blocks of modern life in the Indian urban centers crisscrossing the subcontinent.

The Age of Speculation, Expansion, and Inversion also paralleled the Age of Late Electronics Industry, which itself has been characterized by its propensity to churn out natural monopolies and wipe out swathes of small businesses. Late Electronics Industry's legacy of monopolized communication platforms plays into the seismic shifts taking place in the realm of governance, as we shall see.

Thus, the era since 1970 has been characterized by the Age of Supranational Polity, the Age of Speculation, Expansion, Inversion, and the Late Electronics Industry, and in the Age of post-Darwin, most importantly, the consolidation of Liberalism in the larger portion of society.

To sum up: in the Age of the Nation-state, beginning with the Age of Modernization, the fall in share of the people of faith, first among the intellectuals, and then among the public, paralleled the rise of Liberalism. But by 1973, the end of the Age of Modernization meant the arrival of the Age of Supranational Polity to accommodate the Age of Speculation, Expansion, and Inversion, supported by the remodeled state – the protectionist state – and enabled and encouraged by Liberalism and the liberal ideals, which in addition, since the time it rose to dominance in the society during the Age of Modernization, oversaw the contraction of the Western Civilization including the receding of the West in the Western hemisphere and about which we'll turn next.

The Decline of Western dominance in the Western Domain

If the decline of the West in the non-Western territory may be traced to the year 1917– the year Russia broke away from the West, the decline of the West in the historically Western region has been a long march that began in the aftermath of Second World War, but to this effect the circumstances turned incredibly ripe just as the Age of Modernization ended and support from the liberal elite and the liberal public, even a small share of the overall population, strengthened.

To recall in brief terms, society's liberalization as advocated by liberalism lies in the eradication of all of traditional groupings and the identities. The implicit mechanism through which this is carried out is the invariable, unceasing identification of people of the lower strata of society, manifesting the same in the promotion of ideals of "equality" and "justice" and bringing people into liberal fold. Liberals therefore are employed in the task of redressing the state, which upon assuming the chance springs into action conceiving in myriad decisions that affect society at-large. As a result traditional identities of the people come under attack, including but not limited to nation, race, religion, marriage, gender etc.

Since the doctrine contends that the existence of bad institutions is the cause of the existence of bad society, therefore, by extension, it is also the cause of the existence of the people of the lower strata of society. With an incredible logic of noteworthiness, Liberalism exculpates the culprit for the crimes and the poor for their personal responsibility to their current status, and thereby shifts the responsibility for their actions to bad institutions. Incredibly, todays' descendants of the ancestral people that enacted those institutions and enforced them in the past deserve all the blame.

That is, today's bad people have no personal responsibility for their actions, since they have turned bad only due to the existence of bad institutions. But, the people who are the descendants of those people that enacted these bad institutions long time ago do end up getting all the blame.

The eradication of traditional groupings invariably begins by the exaggeration of identity, its consequences, its dangers, and how it is keeping the society bad. It becomes a contradiction within the Liberal fold that the fight to eradicate traditional identity of the people boils down primarily to blaming the historically oppressing group, deemed to be that way by the very same liberals. Thus, in the process of pitting the oppressing group against the rest of the people, differences among them shall be vastly exacerbated.

Demanding "equality" and "justice" for the people of the lower strata, a useful psychological tool employed by the liberal public in the erosion and destruction of traditional identities and people is forceful revisionism of all things that can serve the purpose at hand. Redefining identity, revising history, undermining cultural practices with false pretense of causing offense to minorities usually take the form.

The fruits of the dilution of nation state from the economic standpoint come from the identity-deprived factors of production (capital, labor, source of raw materials), on the production side (less operating costs); and the expansion of the market, on the distribution side (more revenue).

First, the dilution of nation state – the easiest one to undermine because it is the last in the list of oldest human institutional creations – is duly carried out by the state, advocated by the liberal elite who make up a significant portion of the state– in the administrative, legislature and elected executive sphere, and backed by liberal society, through immigration programs of non-Western people who do not share western values or do not assimilate into western culture, thereby contributing to eroding the longstanding values and identity of the Western people in the shortest time. The support for this program from the liberal society comes to show the loudest not when it is being carried out, but when it comes under attack.

Many Western countries since the 1970s opened their borders, issued visas, and welcomed people from around the world. The then winding down of the colonial enterprise of the West itself, due to the effect of the decline of the West in the non-Western domain, turned out to be a significant source for the people of non-Western origin for Western emigration.

As people of non-Western origin emigrated to the West, there was the necessity for them to be accommodated into Western society as they were without assimilation. Therefore the Liberal creed churned out for the purpose the temporary carryout-mechanisms, the liberal slogans, one may say, that had come to be carrying somewhat with it a kind of force equivalent to a state decree. Hence, one such liberal slogan in that direction that received strong backing from the liberal elite, exhibited through the control of institutional brain trust, is "multiculturalism."

Following the nation state, the erosion of the other oldest institutions as marriage (or family of a husband and a wife), and of the most natural of all, gender (male and female). The identity of husband and wife, and that of male and female, encapsulated in those institutions comes under attack.

In the service of the erosion of the institution of marriage, the definition of marriage, like all other identities, had undergone a convoluted transformation under the liberal lens to be interpreted quite differently. To this effort, a false pretense among the liberal elite for the care of the people of the lower strata of the society springs into action. The Media and the Arts prove extremely useful to this effort, to the undermining of the institutions at hand, and to indoctrinating the liberal public for the same purposes.

In the same vein, the efforts to erode masculinity from men and femininity from women come to life. To this effect, the reinforcement of the ideas as institutional oppression of women by men (the patriarchy in no small part a thing of the past that belongs to the things to be eradicated whether it is actually present today or not), institutional undercutting by men of women across myriad spheres of life and work, whether true in practice or not, and the active work of the liberal public in practice to redress this oppression combines to undermine the traditional character of men and women. The efforts to erode the institution of marriage means the employment of the same-old liberal slogans to that effect – achieving "equality" and "justice" to those groups of people, proving excellent service to the task at hand.

Thus, the stage of multiculturalism had been duly followed by what came to be called "diversity." Diversity, not just of culture but of all kinds of social identities– precisely the type of liberal contradiction trying to eradicate traditional identity but all the while, over the short-term period, reinforces the identity of all of them, either in good light or bad light by labeling and other means.

Peace, Violence & War

Modern Liberalism's unique feature that powerfully captures the people is the ideal of the care for the lower strata of the society. But just as always the ultimately preferred identity to a consummate liberal transcends, so long as there remains one, the traditional norms of division such as family, nation, culture, the liberals ultimately see the human spectrum so far an extent that it does not exclude any humans, which means taking the stock of humanity as a whole.

It may be of noteworthy that the more recent, young liberals, magnifying the epic unfolding of Liberalism, blurt out "Humanism" or "Human Rights" as answer for what they stand for and believe in. It is only natural that the liberals associate themselves with, or believe in such rights for, anything that transcends the traditional identities such as nation and encompass no further exclusion of anyone outside it. "Humanity," "Equal Rights," "Global Citizens," "World Citizens," and other iteration of the same meaningless phrases and utterances with unfettered belief become familiar and even trendy.

Therefore what on the surface appears to be a struggle for "world peace" really underlies liberals' apprehension for and opposition to conflict and war. The alternative, if one is necessary to the combat style of fighting, as evidenced and practiced by the liberals, has been reluctant push for "diplomacy and condemnation," so long such rhetoric-war is devoid of any threats of use of force, even if the rhetoric from the enemy on the other side is not.

From the liberal optics, it becomes familiar to the liberal to despise those harming the vulnerable directly, or indirectly, intentionally, or not, and hence the liberals' clear and vehement opposition to military conflict or even to the escalation of rhetoric. To the liberal, the non-violence stance applies only to foreign wars, as internal or domestic violence (so long there exists grounds to make such a distinction) still remains the avowed technique or the feature of the twentieth century Left. The worship of the street to escalate conflict, or resort to street violence has been an irredeemable tactic of the Left in the style of the French Revolution going into the twenty-first century as well. As the violence of the revolutionary mob during the French Revolution remains an ultimate glorified (and justified) thing of the past.

Specifically modern wars – foreign wars, that is – to the modern liberal always reminisces the nationalistic, or the neo-colonial spirit gone rogue – just another reason to eradicate those arbitrary boundaries of nations and the cultures that define them. Anti-Vietnam war stance in the US during the late 1960s and early 1970s still remains very popular. In fact only after the US fought the invading Iraqi Army in the Gulf War in the early 1990s – with the swiftness of the mission that undoubtedly helped – that the anti-war syndrome in the US descendant from the Vietnam days had been shrugged off. In regards to the Iraq war, it may be noted that irrespective of the enormous economic burdens due to the war that befell the country, or the primary grounds for entering the war in the first place remain shaky, the liberal Left always, always, in its heart opposes war– poor economics, or, lack of evidence is just one more reason to stand opposed.

Chapter Six

Critical Analysis of Classical Liberalism

Liberalism and Economy

The doctrine of Liberalism from late eighteenth and nineteenth centuries had transformed the state into liberal state, and in addition had advocated laissez-faire policy on the part of liberal state. At the turn of the twentieth century, laissez-faire-economics-guided liberal state had been remodeled into interventionist liberal state, and then, importantly, over the course of the century into protectionist state.

Despite the fact that in the real world laissez-faire-economics turned out to be grossly inept at best and suicidal at worst— so much so that the doctrine had to make a significant correction, mainstream economists of the twentieth century, especially those in the mold of neoclassical style, had undertaken extraordinary efforts to theoretically prove the stability and the durability of such an economic system, or, in other words, to conclusively show the wisdom of having the laissez-faire-economics state.

As a matter of great deal, to put mildly, the nineteenth century laissez-faire economics was a dud. The idea of Self-regulating market as the best economic structure for all parties, as advocated by Classical Liberalism, is a fallacy because the nature of economic actors it supposes does not correspond to the real world that partly consists of fictitious commodities. The reason why laissez-faire economics had proved to be so devastating to workers and businesses in the nineteenth century and in the first three decades of the twentieth century was because it was grotesquely irrelevant to real world. And that was so because of the fact that laissez-faire economics was developed prior to the advent of the Age of Industrial Revolution. Simply, laissez-faire-economics was a product of pre-Industry, agrarian economy.

The Age of Industrial Revolution greatly expanded the variety of goods traded internationally not least of all the many inventions that were technologically complex and expensive. With the advent of heavy industry, the diffusion of technology especially across the Atlantic through international trade was a common phenomenon. That is why an expanding volume of international trade since 1860 created a need for a new, trustworthy system for conducting international trade and investment. The International Gold Standard, existing for some time, had come to serve that need.

The Self-regulating market in the domestic economy and the International Gold Standard, that together caused persistent unemployment and sporadic deflationary spirals, had proved catastrophic. The effects it had on the lives of labor in Europe may have been a critical factor in creating the semi-emergency conditions that allowed the radical political parties in Europe during the 1930s to eclipse to power, that then paved way for them to morph into dictatorship. In Germany, additionally, woes from the Peace Treaty had fueled the rage and fierceness for retribution and no doubt had contributed to the rise of the National Socialist Workers Party, which detested Self-regulating Capitalism and all the people they deemed responsible for the abhorrent conditions the country had supposedly found in.

The Liberal doctrine was blind to the realities of having the Self-regulating market and the affects it has on the lives of capitalists and workers alike. Capitalism of the time, due to the effects of Self-regulating market, was unstable at best. The correction the doctrine had to make after the disastrous consequences it had unleashed, including but not limited to its paving the way for the rise of evil, anti-capitalist, mass-murdering ideologies across Europe and Japan, should have had severely undercut its standing in the eyes of posterity.

Until mid-twentieth century, the creation of central banks in the United States and across Europe and Latin America was the deemed solution to rein-in the shortfalls stemming from the International Gold Standard. The downturns spared no one, including the Industrial-capitalists and all other businesses. Although central banks existed in few European countries for well over a hundred years before the turn of the twentieth century, their functions were limited in the scope and included mainly the financing of war.

As the Great Depression unleashed misery and ruin in the urban and rural centers, only by getting off the Gold Standard, which itself had played a pivotal role in spreading and worsening the Depression, had each industrial country halted the economy from digging further into slump and started recovery. The decision on the part of industrial nations to get on board the Gold Standard again after the end of the Great War, as the system during the War had operated tenuously, was a major blunder as Winston Churchill himself later attested somewhat differently in regards to the United Kingdom. We'll learn about the causes of the Great Depression later on, in the context of the 2008 financial crisis, and also how the Gold Standard worsened that situation.

After the end of the Great War, the British economist John Maynard Keynes (1883 – 1946) strongly advocated that Britain should stay out of the Gold Standard. From 1925 – the year Great Britain reentered the International Gold Standard – the works of Keynes, who detested Socialism, on the whole constituted a vigorous defense of Capitalism – or to state more specifically a defense of Capitalism to preserve the private enterprise element of the system but not the kind of Self-regulating market of Capitalism that defined the previous century. Keynes was thinking hard about the severe unemployment problem in Britain that lasted throughout the 1920s, with one million to one-and-a-quarter million Britons out of work at any time in the decade. Even prior to 1928 the central banks of the two Anglo-Saxon countries headed in the US by Benjamin Strong (1872 – 1928) who died on the job and Montagu Norman (1871 – 1950) in the UK coordinated to keep the US interest rates low amidst flagging British pound.

In this theatre of worsening conditions throughout the 1920s Keynes had come to doubt the virtuosity of the Self-regulating market – a concept he was mightily familiar with since his student days learning mathematics, philosophy, economics– the latter two mostly self-taught, at King's College, Cambridge; the fall of the market economy into depression and its inability to self-correct only strengthened his conviction that the notion of self-regulating market was dubious. Keynes therefore recommended to the British government 1) that Britain should jump off of the Gold Standard, and 2) government intervention (by deficit spending) to rein in the persisting unemployment in the domestic economy.

In the early 1930s only as the Depression worsened that Britain finally left the Gold Standard in 1931 (see on YouTube Keynes' brief remarks after the decision was made public). The reeling effects from the crisis still afflicted the country as more than three to three-and-a-half million were unemployed in 1932. The decline in the industrial production hit the bottom in 1932 and began to move upwards from the following year onwards.

The Austrian economist Fredrick Von Hayek (1899 – 1992), who also detested Socialism but had a reputation for idolizing absolute free-markets (Self-regulating markets), contented that government intervention in the economy is harmful at best in the short term and is the road to serfdom in the long run – apparently because the government's intervention in the economy is a form of coercion on the individual, thus paving the way toward totalitarianism. The two economists were at war. Keynes' short and blunt response to Hayek's supposedly false contention was that in a liberal democracy government intervention in the economy does not lead to totalitarianism.

Even today, scholars cannot fully and correctly reconcile these two economists and their views on government intervention and the consequences such a move may have on other aspects. But the solution to correct the then state of affairs and the impact it shall have in the short haul and the long haul is nuanced, as we'll see shortly, and that both of them the great economic thinkers of the twentieth century they were neither entirely correct or incorrect.

But, one aspect of those times that is irrefutable was that the economies of the West were unstable at best, and were plagued with obstinate problems of persisting unemployment at worst. In fact, Keynes correctly diagnosed the problem plaguing the Self-regulating markets of Capitalism across the West, and precisely and logically identified why the Self-regulating market had failed, and would continue to fail to create full-employment.

Hayek unmistakably and flagrantly misinterpreted the Keynesian idea of deficit spending and wise monetary policy to stabilize the Self-regulating markets and create full-employment. With the benefit of hindsight, reconciling the two is easy now. It was by not acting on the Keynesian ideas that in fact would have paved the way for totalitarianism just as Hayek contended but not for the causes he supposed Keynes's designs were, which was government takeover of the economy or something close to that effect.

That is, by not acting on the Keynesian ideas to bring the affairs of the economy to stability in the midst of the worst economic crisis that had fueled the rise of Fascism, as it had in many of the continental European countries. Do nothing– the essential Hayek mantra at that time was a recipe for disaster.

Therefore, Hayek's statement that government intervention in the economy is the road to serfdom in the long run is not true, provided that the government intervention is limited to Keynes' prescription to fix the Self-regulating market. Where Hayek turns out correct is on the nature of government intervention in the economy, and that is where Keynes' response to Hayek's original contention turns out to be incorrect.

We can surely conclude that the type of intervention that Keynes suggested would not lead to totalitarianism. If anything, it was the lack of such intervention that would have led to it. It is the type of intervention that involves the government takeover of vast swathes of the economy that even in the most liberal democracy in the long run displays signs of totalitarianism, just as Hayek correctly predicted.

The fact remains that Hayek firmly held on to the nineteenth century style laissez-faire economics, whose failure was part of the reason his home country had been run over by the neighboring Nazis. Britain, the home of Keynes, remained a free country were it not for timely stabilization of the British economy by leaving the Gold Standard.

The conditions in Germany only worsened, as it never really left the crippling monetary system, partly due to the fears of hyperinflation that decimated its economy in 1923 and the same fear that continue to haunt it to this day and age. When Britain suspended the Gold Standard in September 1931, the sterling exchange rate fell by a whopping 25% that effectively triggered the complete collapse of the German foreign trade. France and the US were the only two countries that remained relatively unconstrained in their Gold reserves in those turbulent times, as Gold escaped to whichever country that was deemed safest and trustworthy.

The US was the only large western country that did not suffer from the economic burdens carried over from the Great War and therefore remained relatively free from foreign debts and currency inflation, while France stabilized its currency (gold reserve/currency) by 1926. The stabilization was later codified into a 1928 Monetary Law that fixed the lower bound at 35%. But interestingly both countries sterilized the gold inflows, effectively not creating as much money through the banking system as the gold reserves allowed.

The two countries, but especially France, sucked out the world gold reserves just before and after the 1929 crash. The gold reserves of the entire world had increased by 24% in December 1932 from December 1927. However, France had unmistakably taken in every ounce of new gold during that period, as it saw its gold reserves grow from 7% of the world reserves in 1926 to 27% in 1932. The deflationary pressure caused by the abnormal redistribution of gold had effectively crippled the world. So much inflow of gold would have ceased to be a problem had France and to a lesser extent the US monetized the gold inflow. That was an astounding development having enormous ripple effects throughout the West, and whose significance was neglected until very recently when a working paper was published in 2010 shining light on the role of France in causing the Great Depression.

Fascism, Nazism, Communism and Anarchy

The evil ideologies – Fascism, Nazism and Communism – that produced the cruelty on the European continent before and during the Second World War are the exemplars of aggressive, state-controlled, totalitarian regimes. These ideologies differ critically in the type of fervor that fueled their ascent to power but they all arose, in theory or in practice, from the failed liberal democratic politics of the nineteenth century.

Whereas Communism in its rise fueled rage and garnered support to its mission from the labor to beat in the supposed class warfare, Fascism and Nazism provoked national fervor among the same not only in the rise to power but also in the war efforts because they believed national identity ranked supreme to any pseudo-class struggle among men and for which they would fight for and sacrifice their life. Even the Communist USSR's nationalistic fervor displayed in such phrases as "Mother Russia" played heavily into the spirit to drumbeat into fighting the enemy.

At the core of the identity, Fascism and Communism are near identical, except that the former allows the capitalist-businessmen and other elites to own property, mainly by co-opting after the rise and becoming essential to its function. Their similarity comes out unambiguously in the totalitarian tendencies prevalent in their philosophy and in practice. Both echo the same features: state-control of everything especially the press, freedom of speech abridgement, external aggression, appetite for conquering foreign lands, permanent state of emergency, and large-scale murder. Fascism is what one gets by implementing Socialism in a capitalist country, just as one gets Communism by doing the same in a non-capitalist agricultural country. The men doing it in either type of country identify similarly: they are all socialists. As it often comes to this: Fascism and Communism are different without distinction.

But Nazism critically differs from Fascism; it is just that the Nazi governance interweaves and shares parallels with the Fascist state-society structure such as the control of everything. However Nazism, Fascism and Communism, besides being totalitarian and sharing the same intellectual wellspring, have another thing in common: it is their path to power. All three ideologies adopted and improved on the Sorel's notion of the power of the myth and the usefulness of violence to seize and consolidate power. The path to power was not in the line of Gramsci's long march of the institutions, but in the manner of selling a Sorel-style myth to the masses, confronting opposition with violence. After seizing power they decimated the cultural and political institutions – naturally to never allow the sway of family and religion in regards to the individual and of democracy in regards to the opposition – in the line of Gramsci's idea but for the sake of consolidation of power with the given advantage of doing it in much shorter time.

As it comes to the Nazi Germany's actions, a dissection into two relevant components has to be made to understand the interweaving of ideologies and forces: the ambitions to colonize the European continent, and the Holocaust. Both interweave in the execution. The colonization of the continent progresses in parallel to the extermination of Jews on the conquered lands. It is the first action – the case to acquire colonies at any cost, whether they were in the African continent or in the European landmass – that shares parallels with Italian Fascism including the conditions in the respective nations that allowed their rise. It is in the second action that the distinction starkly appears.

Jews served in the Italian government and the Italian Fascist Party all the way until Mussolini's Italy implemented the race laws in 1938 and at which point the Jews were expelled. The laws in Italy were never enforced with the cruelty and barbarity anywhere close to that of Nazi Germany. It was only after the Nazis had invaded northern Italy and created a puppet state in Salo by the name Italian Social Republic (most of the Northern and Central Italy with German support) in 1943 that the Jews in Italy were rounded up.

Fascism had little to do with anti-Semitism until Hitler. Through the 1920s and going into the 1930s Fascism was seen as something different, as a new form of governance to be aspired to and modeled on, as did the Left in the US. The anti-Semitism component of Nazism is what most starkly distinguishes the ideology from Fascism. Anti-Semitism of Nazi Germany and the Holocaust that resulted may be called Hitlerism and this together with the infusion of fascist governance style – that being socialism in a capitalist country – is the resulting ideology that is Nazism as displayed in practice. The above dissection and comparison is a rough approximation of the actual events to serve the purpose of analysis, as brutal regimes such as those operate with fervent ideology that normality ceases to exist.

But the liberal intellectuals at the end of the Second World War struggled to come to grips with the tainted evil ideologies on the Left that were bent on World control. Fascism and National Socialism, the latter tainted with Holocaust and the former with its associations and parallels with the latter, were ideologies to distance away. The liberal dream of eradicating the traditional identities, such as the nation-state, found an ally in the historical drama at the end of the Second World War. As the early steps of the beloved projects of International Cooperation in the name of Human Rights were brought to fruition, right there Liberalism severed, swiftly and surreptitiously, long-standing associations with national identity. Nation-state, supposedly, has been a traditional mode of living and an elusive creature of the naïve and old-minded, since then and now, to the liberal mind. And therefore, since the end of the War those who associate with national identity and those subscribing to the political parties that uphold it, according to the liberal edicts, belonged to the other side of the political spectrum. And also, somewhat cunningly, in the extension of the Liberal logic, naturally, they all belonged to the anti-liberal faction, including the people and parties from before the end of the War.

For an analogy, consider the institution of marriage. The Left in the West also believed in the traditional concept of marriage until it no longer did. Nation and national identity, like marriage, did not initially belong to either side of the political spectrum because they never were political. But both have been institutions of creation – the latter old enough to have its origins traced to time immemorial and the former successful enough to see about two hundred of them across the World.

As is the case, people on the Left and the Right all were nationalists, until the Left no longer was. People on the Left and the Right all believed in traditional marriage, until the left no longer did. The tactic to slide and project what it stopped to believe onto the other side proved useful historically. And just like that, the two evil ideologies Fascism and Nazism have been moved from the Left of the political spectrum to the Right – a task made easy due to the manipulation by the International Socialists, as we'll see, and happily played along after Second World War by the Left across the West.

In the struggle for power to decimate the failed liberal democratic politics for the one last time the socialist parties of the Marxist type encountered opposition from their own ex-party members who had reorganized under the national banner of socialism. The National Socialists in Germany and the Italian Fascists in Italy started to beat the Socialists at their own game of intimidation.

The counter-reaction from these Socialist parties (that echoed the Moscow Party line) was to start spewing propaganda that their opponents were the last vestige of fight-back by the capitalists against the Socialists, wholly in accord with Karl Marx's long-standing prediction that was further underscored later by Lenin. Also, in order to shame those parties and their members, be they current or probable, the Socialist international propagandists had begun to label those opposition parties as belonging to the Right of the political spectrum, as it naturally followed that any opposition to them did not belong to the Left of the spectrum.

It is from this welt of relentless worldwide propaganda spewed by the International Socialists that the Fascist and National Socialist parties have come to be perceived to this day as belonging to the Right – a nice piece of propaganda advantage enjoyed by liberal historians writing after the War about the transformative events of the century. They have succeeded in pushing under the rug the connections shared by the twentieth century Progressivism or its offspring successor Modern Liberalism with those ideologies.

Whereas Communism explicitly sought the support of the lower strata of society in the mode of a class warfare against the supposed profiteers, Liberalism – which also upholds its commitment to the very same class of people as Communism and always understood as belonging to the Left – could never have moved away from the close ties it has had and continue to have with this variety of evil ideology.

To the Left, the Nationalism part of National Socialism may be corrupted to slide and obfuscate the connection the ideology has had with the side. Often columnists and writers regurgitate the leftist concocted story that the Nazis only called themselves socialists because they tried to win over the socialists and that they were nationalists first and foremost. For one, even if this story is taken at face value, how can it ever be proved that nationalism before the advent of the Second World War belonged to the Right and not to the Left. As it was clear, until the end of the Second World War everyone was nationalist in the traditional meaning of the word – this qualification is necessary because liberal writers for the past fifty years have come to pervert the term nationalism for it to mean fascism.

For all of history recounted thus far, if anything is apparent it is that nationalism in the original traditional meaning had nothing to do with the evil cruelties of the West. Fascism was that form of socialism that had had the possibility to be turned into reality; that had had the best chance for it to be made true in practice. As Mussolini realized in the aftermath of the collapse of the international variety of socialism, if the tactics and mission were confined within a single state – a single state because the Sorel tactics can be put to effect. Sorel's tactics of the revolutionary use of violence by the insurgents was the strongest abrogation of the state's monopoly on force, and thus to the causing of the destabilization of the state thereafter and to the paving of anything that can replace it. Thus Lenin, Mussolini and Hitler were inspired from and followed the Sorel's tactics and mounted revolutionary coup against the provisional and lawful government and wherever it helped they co-opted the democratic elements of the country. A good clue in identifying the revolutionary character gripping any side of the political spectrum is by noting what front the group that practices violence falls into. As was the case, violence (other than the state), and mass control (myth) had always belonged to the Left and together had inhabited the tendencies of revolution.

Thus Fascism was the closest to the realization of socialism right then and there. Whereas the penultimate causes of the Second World War lay in the foreign aggression of the Nazi and Fascist regimes, the cause of the aggression itself was a feature of historical, economical, geographical, and political circumstances, as we have seen in Chapter Four. When Great Britain and France held colonies that spanned the globe, foreign aggression of the Nazi, Fascist and Japanese militarist regimes was thus an extension of the colonial enterprise – but on the European continent in the case of Germany – hence the reference as the Late Age of Colonial Expansion. The cause of the Holocaust again leads back to anti-Semitism of the Nazis, and henceforth the primary characterizing feature of it.

The corruption of the term "nationalism" in theory and in practice since the end of the Second World War to mean fascism had indirectly contributed, of significant advantage to the liberal cause, in the effort and spirit to erase national borders, dilute national identity. Just as we have recounted here, it was the element of foreign aggression within the context of the Age of Colonial Expansion (or rather an extension of it) that collided forces with the allied powers. Germany, Italy and Japan all displayed foreign aggression and invaded countries throughout the 1930s. The British government, desperately trying to avoid war with Germany, had tried to appease Adolf Hitler up until the Munich Pact concluded in September 1938 that permitted the German annexation of Sudetenland– a portion of Czechoslovakia inhabited by the German people and a legacy of the dissolution of the Austro-Hungarian Empire. Thus the momentum during the decade of 1930s was one of annexation, conquering and control, with various motives and reasons sagging the minds of the conquering warlords.

The liberal leftist writers through a sleight of hand had obfuscated the origins of the regimes that we call Nazism, Fascism, and Militarism to the benefit of the Left. This level of intellectual dishonesty is quite dangerous for the manifestly simple reason that it is only by clearly learning about the evils can the rise of evil in all of the original or derivative forms be noted, identified, and prevented from ever showing up again.

Totalitarian tendencies originate, and have always arisen, on the Left, which harbors ideologies that at extreme seeks state control of every facet of human life, whether it is economic, social, or personal in character. Thus, Fascism and Nazism, which share parallels in their desire to seek ultimate state control of everything, just like the case of Communism, belong squarely to the Left. The extreme Right, where ultimate freedom from the state is the dream, leads to anarchy, not fascism. That is, the diminished state necessarily leads to the collapse of society, and therefore, chaos ensues in the place of civilization. The outcome, due to the descent to the extreme Right, is contrary to the one arising due to descent to Fascism and Nazism, where full-state control is the dream. Nevertheless, even the origins of anarchy in practice are not what it appears to be at the first glance.

Practically, even anarchy originates from and belongs to the Left. As in when an extremely liberal society marches forward with an extremely liberal state, as evidenced in practice when Modern Liberalism is in the peak of its unfolding, the law and order of the country collapses because the liberal state engages liberally or leniently only with a certain section of the society. The same liberal state engages aggressively against another, causing to ignore the laws of the land and in time worsening such a trend.

Technically, anarchy seems to belong to the Right, which in its extreme as understood seeks maximum individual freedom from the state. However, technically, where there is no state to allow for unabashed freedom (zero state-coercion), there essentially is no civilization. That it is with an assumption that civilization is enabled by the existence of the state, the Right-to-Left political spectrum came to light. And in that correct technical sense, the Right seeks minimal state control of the individual (and that means of the economy as well) and the Left, maximum. Thus, it is in that understanding that the Left by being overtly liberal to certain sections of the society lays the path to anarchy.

Therefore, in a civilized society, technically or practically, anarchy originates on the Left. It may be noted that civilized society duly vanishes as lawlessness begins, unless of course an intervention to this state of affairs in any shape or form is possible.

Anarchy is such a state of affairs where one arrives due to the ignorance of the laws of the land. The liberal elite urging the liberal state to ignore the law carries with it the risk of an eventual breakdown of law and order, culminating in the making of one's own laws, which is the very definition of anarchy. The US federal government refusing to enforce immigration laws of the land for few decades now, or laws prohibiting gun ownership by certain individuals such as criminals, or laws concerning white-collar crime – qualify as examples.

Even if the laws of the land are duly changed by the legislature to accommodate the same (being liberal in the action to criminals), thereby removing the feature that we termed "ignorance of the law," one still cannot escape the inevitable outcome (resulting from the acts now allowed by the law), which is the breakdown of order, and if anything, such a move shall only make the outcome of disorder arrive that much faster and worse. This condition means that even if the legislature is not fully liberal to co-opt with the liberal executive, there shall be an outcome no different than the one that was outlined prior.

Chapter Seven

Critical Analysis of Modern Liberalism

The Curious Case of the Liberal Elite

A critical analysis of Modern Liberalism shall remain incomplete without understanding the strange creature called the "liberal elite" that so thoroughly underpins and provides the impetus to the success of liberal ideology. The liberal elite is a group of liberals who by virtue of position exercise power and influence over the rest. In our times, they make up a majority in state administration, politics, media, academia, etc. Their origins can be traced to the Great Awakening itself in the latter part of the nineteenth century. And they crucially represent a link to the eighteenth century enlightenment, and hence a carryover of the enlightenment thinking and ideas. Their predecessors in the Ancién Regime were not those who shaped the enlightenment but those who belonged to the aristocracy, or the nobility – a small group of people of the privileged class exercising authority and influence over the rest.

The rise of the liberal elite during the twentieth century has been enabled to a large extent by the restructured interventionist state. The big government replaced small government, and the bureaucracy to support the new behemoth expanded as well. Government spending as a percent of GDP increased vastly, as a result.

The boundless energy of the early enthusiasts to make an impact on the world had come to shape the course of events from then onwards. The interventionist state itself was a product of the Great Awakening and a making of the early modern liberals, and as such the liberal elite's outsized influence has manifestly expanded ever since. The outpost that relentlessly churned out the people who made into those ranks was none other than the central piece in the tool of Liberalism to influence the world – Education. Mainly, it was higher education. Higher education enriched and nurtured the so-called "human capital" of which the liberal elite claims their economic and social value. The University has been the backbone and the perfect filter and the spring pad that worked to that effect.

It was the eighteenth century science presaging the nineteenth century upgrade that acted as the backbone of the late nineteenth century Industrial Revolution that gave the world the electrical and mechanical engineer. In similar vein, it was the eighteenth and nineteenth century political science and philosophy that acted as the backbone of the late nineteenth century Great Awakening that gave the world the social engineer. As such, the tide of that momentum carried over into the twentieth century saw its first triumph in one instance that starkly stands out. That was the precipitous rise in the world of politics of the political scientist with a Ph.D. in Political Science, Woodrow Wilson (1856 – 1924), who managed to chart a whole new course for the United States under his presidency.

But at the core, the most critical support structure that helped propel, fund, and sustain the liberal elite was the process of modernization itself, which was a gift of the industrial revolution. The modernization of traditional economic activities allowed the incomes of workers in those industries to grow proportionately. Importantly, such service industries as education, public administration, media and entertainment, which act as a hub for the liberal elites, had been shaped by and benefited from the modernization program directly and indirectly. The urbanization and the city culture resulting from the modernization have also had notable impact in shaping them. Higher education was the filter pad, the urban city was the choice of location, and big government was the source of income.

The nature of the liberal elite is best captured by author Nassim Nicholas Taleb in a recent essay titled "The Intellectual Yet Idiot" that is part of his larger upcoming book *Skin in the Game* (2018). Taleb describes the Intellectual Yet Idiot, shortened to IYI, as a group of people assuming roles in bureaucracy, politics, media, and academia, and who have no-skin-in-the-game. The IYI is called thus because he embodies a unique combination of particular skills or the lack thereof. The IYI is the gifted writer who can easily pass tests prepared and scored by people like them. The IYI can write the most interesting piece on any task, but when it comes to doing it himself, he is utterly incompetent. The IYIs are highly educated and intelligent but have no practical knowledge. As an example, they could write an excellent piece on how to fix a broken window, or to change a tire, but should one of their gets broken or has a flat tire, they would have to rely on professional help. But those intellectual experts with degrees from elite institutions are the self-appointed members of a club with the desire to tell the rest how to live, work and think. Bureaucrats make regulations for industries they had never worked in; journalists write pieces on the things they have no clue. They look down on large swaths of people who have no credible degrees from elite institutions.

The world as perceived by the liberal elite and the role they envision in it springs from their elite education. The liberal elite carry an air of superiority in their abilities and intellect; live on a false authority to lecture and dictate how everything should be; and assume without skepticism that everyone lives based on their standards and beliefs. They are philosopher-kings in the mold of Woodrow Wilson. Perhaps that may be the reason why the former president Wilson, notwithstanding his history of overt racism and contempt for the constitution, is held in high regard and often ranked by historians who themselves are liberals at the top of the list of the greatest US presidents.

The critical contribution of the liberal elite has nonetheless resided not in the specific outcomes of the job, but the role they played and continue to play in the liberalization of society. The liberal elite has been the torchbearer of Modern Liberalism, carrying and sustaining the intellectual legacy of the Great Awakening all the way into the twenty-first century. Their world outlook stems from their desire to create heaven on earth, and everything they do and advocate for is a step in that direction for them. To see the society evolve in that utopian direction is their self-assigned mission. They know how best to organize the society.

But what has been their real contribution to the development of the condition of life? Has it been significant enough to afford them the privilege to tell the rest what to do or how to think or who to vote? Taleb's examination of their record puts them squarely in the incompetent box. He notes the IYI has been wrong on numerous subjects at several times in multitude ways. Here, with the help of original analysis of economic system undertaken in the previous Chapters, we can arrive at a different kind of examination of their contribution and of the contribution of mass education programs.

The spree of inventions of the Industrial Revolution between 1870 and 1913, as shown in Fig. 3.2, had resulted in the formation of final goods heavy industry, and precisely, new sub-sector industries within the heavy industry division. The numerous discoveries in Chemistry, and the discoveries of chemical processes, such as the Haber-Bosch synthesis of Ammonia that was first used on an industrial scale in 1913, have all presaged the rise of the liberal elite. In fact, the inventors and discoverers, and most often the businessmen who commercialized them, were mightily different compared to the liberal elite. The former has had useful practical knowledge in abundance, while the latter none. The former grew up and worked in rural towns; the latter was a creation of the city.

While the Industrial Revolution had ended hundred years ago, the stark contrast that underlies between those two kinds of people may be discernable even among the prominent people that shaped the Late Electronics Industry. Steve Jobs for all the eccentricities known and written about him had a family that was not much different from the bygone age. His parents Paul and Clara Jobs were less affluent and had modest jobs. Steve growing up learned the importance of practical knowledge, understood and appreciated design from his father. His parents did not force him to clinch elite degrees. With only modest amount saved for college, he nevertheless joined an elite liberal arts college in Portland, Oregon against his parents' wishes. Having soon realized the under-utility of such a costly degree, he eventually dropped out. Education, as it was imparted, did not seem promising, as it had failed to help him see a future. That path came differently for him. To Jobs, education did not have to begin and end on College campuses; he firmly believed education was not a stopgap measure but a lifelong ordeal, or more like a joyous journey to relish. Despite the early mistakes from which he had never ceased to learn, the practical approach to doing anything, the wisdom of the humble allowed him to see things without the hollowness of megalomania that comes with the twentieth century education. That attitude and that approach had helped him to understand and pursue opportunities when none seemed to exist in the minds of rival firms' executives who all had elite degrees.

To revert to the main point, industrialization gifted machinery and equipment that upon installation modernized all of the other traditional economic activities. That brings us to the popular conception, stemming from the imagination of liberals, of the significance of education to the development of a country. Since the twentieth century was the education-century, and most of the modernization and the resulting high incomes also a peculiarity of the twentieth century, the correlation between the two phenomena appear almost hundred-percent. To the liberal elite, there is little skepticism as to the tremendous contribution of education. It's almost as if the higher education of twentieth century entirely caused the breakthroughs of the industrial world.

The line of thinking that underpins that perception is not all too different from that proposed in standard economic theory. To explain the long observed phenomena of the services industries outperforming all else within the GDP composition of a wealthy industrialized country, or in other words the income share of services outperforming all else within the National Income, the standard answer goes like this. During the twentieth century, the low-income individuals (families) prioritized basic consumer goods. But as productivity in those industries the individual worked in went up, he began to earn a higher income. His higher income has purchasing power to demand more goods. However, the individual needed only so many clothes, shoes, and food, fuel, etc. that the spending on consumer goods soon saturated. He then began to demand more services – more and better education and healthcare for his family, regular entertainment, expensive vacations, faster transportation, etc. It was the movement to Phase Two– a more advanced phase, in which individuals and families stock up a basic measure of consumer goods and no more, but demand the provision of unmeasured services of all kinds, the reason why services took up increasingly larger share within the GDP and commanded higher incomes within the National Income over the century. However, both explanations are grossly incorrect.

It was the invention of machinery that upon commercialization and installation in every other industry except for services; and the invention of equipment that upon commercialization and installation in every services industry; and the discovery of chemical elements, compounds, and processes, that propelled every other traditional economic activity into high-income status. In other words, it was the provision of machinery, equipment, or chemical (or metallurgical) process that allowed each industry to produce, provide goods and services at high productivity and low cost. Thus it was that process in which year-after-year since the dawn of the industrial revolution each traditional industry accumulated the machinery and equipment that enabled to push productivity and therefore the income-from-the-production up. Those industries reaped the rewards of technology as embedded in the machinery or equipment that helped them to carry more passengers on the jets that were propelled much faster by gas turbines, or jet engines. Education and training were required to understand, operate or oversee a machine or equipment; and thus education was an outcome or an effect of the real phenomenon. It was not the cause, but rather a consequence that had come to be the requisite element to finish the task.

That blows the myth of human capital (or education) as the most important factor of production in a country, as firmly believed by mainstream economists. That proposition had come to be so ingrained in them that the theory of economic development concerning a backward country became dominated by only one factor and that being "human capital." It's almost as if those skyscrapers in New York City took years and years of rigorous education to get them built.

To sum up, it was the Industrial Revolution alone that was the source of all of the wealth and of high income accumulated and earned respectively in all of the various sections of the three strata of the economy. That conclusion may be reckoned differently. In the last hundred-and-fifty-years, what another extraordinary event the world was the witness of had the power to transform the way the traditional economic activities— farming, forestry, mining, construction, education, healthcare, entertainment, transportation, communication, etc., are performed?

The resulting modernization sparked by industrialization increased the incomes of all industries, and that then ballooned the state coffers. Specifically, the growing incomes meant an increasing share of families in the US over the middle of the twentieth century had become qualified to pay taxes on incomes. Thus in that century, the taxes paid by the top 1% income earners at first made up most of the federal tax inflow. Then in the middle of the century, the increasingly high, high-to-mid, and mid-income earners began to pay taxes, compressing the share of taxes paid by the 1% in the overall taxes. That trend continued until the mid-1970s, precisely until when the process of modernization ended. Since then the trend was the rising share of the taxes paid by top 1%. For the top 1%, their share in the aggregate tax inflow in an annum over the entire century is a bell curve. During this period, the tax inflow increased massively as a percent of national income (or GDP). It was that ballooned state coffers that began to fund a large segment of the liberal elite, especially in Academia, Bureaucracy, and Politics.

That brings back to the question of the importance of education and the contribution of the liberal elite to the advancement of life on earth. We have just explored the fallacies of education and human capital. The significant inventions and discoveries, and the science behind those, which vastly improved the quality of life on earth, had already happened before the idea of progressive education as advocated by the educational reformer John Dewey (1859 – 1952) took hold in the second and third decade of the twentieth century. It was just that education and human capital took credit for the productivity growth when it rightfully belonged to the inventors and discoverers and the businessmen. Education and human capital aren't the ultimate causes; they are the requisite raw materials that go into the machine called modernization.

The final nail in the coffin to the breakdown of the popular misconceptions of education, the human capital, and of the liberal elite is to analyze spending on education and GDP per Capita growth rates. The US spent billions and billions of dollars on education in the decades since the 1960s, and especially so since the 1970s. That spending was unparalleled in history. As evident from Fig. 13.2 (see Chapter Thirteen), the average US GDP per Capita growth rate of 1.86 % for the period 1973 – 2003 did not see an improvement over the average rate of 2.42 % for the period 1950 – 1973. The average rate for the latter part of the century was only a slight improvement over the average rate of 1.61 % for the period 1913 – 1950 that witnessed the Great Depression, and just slightly higher than the average rate of 1.82 % for the period 1870 – 1913 that timed the Industrial Revolution. As compared to the period 1950 – 1973, the decline in GDP per Capita rate during the period 1973 – 2003 despite throwing billions of dollars into education had caused a bewildered economist to ask the question, as reflected in the title of his 1996 economics paper, "where has all the education gone?"

If we have learned anything in this section, it is that GDP per Capita growth has little to do with education. Industrialization and Modernization started and ended before 1974. The Late Electronics Industry came to the fore in the early 1980s and the Internet Industry in the late 1990s that for a few years pushed the growth rate up in the late 1990s only to see it fall back to the norm. That has been how the miracle of technology worked. Therefore, the marvels and glory of the liberal elite and their authority have floated on their false claim to intellectual superiority. Their only real tangible contribution was "words" – just words on paper. Well, how did those words fare?

Having explored the source of vastly improving quality of life through the twentieth century, the source that was neither education in and of itself, nor human capital, what about the quality of the work of the liberal elite? As it turns out, they aren't even rigorous at their game. Having put him in the incompetent box, Taleb in his essay lists out some of the things the IYI has been wrong on, and it includes Iraq, Libya, Syria, urban planning, carbohydrate diets, stochastic equilibrium modeling, housing projects, selfish gene and so on. The liberal elite has been revealed to be incompetent as well – incompetent not just at the practical aspects of life, but even at their game of theorizing and policy-making. That is in regards to the social, political and economic aspects of life, the stewards of liberal thought have been mostly wrong.

Significantly, they have been wrong even on theories devised to spread prosperity from industry and technology, which has never been their creation, to the distant parts of the world outside the West. Mainstream economists over the past few decades have had come to fetish the concept that is "human capital" and the supposed supreme role it plays in attaining prosperity. The theory of rapid economic development – a process involving the construction of millions of modern houses equipped with heavy industry technologies such as washing machines, refrigerators, dishwashers, and the construction of highways, high-speed railways, the accumulation of heavy industry business capital to manufacture machinery, and equipment to provide for all other industries – comes down to more and better education, as per the theory.

Forgotten to them that not only human capital is not capital at all in the correct sense of the term that is "capital," but that more education has failed to have any visible impact in the Western world. Even an overemphasis on education in late-industrializing countries by diverting limited savings, not into light manufacturing, but into education can hold back growth and stifle the process of rapid wealth accumulation. This miserable state of affairs has continued to prevail on the subject of economics of wealthy nations and the economics of developing nations as well. There seemed to exist no certain theory that can guide policymakers in the Global South in their efforts to rapidly develop their nations. It was for that reason I took it upon myself to get to "that" – to discover the relevant general laws and devise the appropriate theory of rapid economic development and the useful mechanisms to make it happen in practice – a task at which mainstream economists have had failed trying over the past seventy years.

Liberalization of Society and its Discontents

The eighteenth century was about the liberalization of state; the nineteenth century about the liberalization of economy; the twentieth century – the liberalization of society.

Modern liberalism, through the liberals, rolls over the task of liberalization of society and worsens the condition of life. But why does Liberalism create such an outcome? Liberalism does so because it does not understand human nature – its pro-reason and anti-tradition stance is antithetical to the existence of a stable and free society.

Liberalism's advocacy for anti-tradition is based upon an axiom with the claim contradicting human nature. That is, the Liberal doctrine's straightforward disdain for and the eradication of all traditional classifications of people, whether the grouping of the people is due to the nature (such as race, or gender) or is the result of evolution of society and the condition of life over centuries or millenniums (such as marriage, nation-state, or religion), contradicts man's natural instinct and impulse for association and group segregation. In fact, nothing could provide more evidence of the natural, unfiltered and uncorrupted kind than that of man's impulse for association – founded upon similarities like shared values, and more specifically along the lines of culture and the morals – to the idea of nation-forming for political organization as one of normalcy.

The Liberal disdain for the traditional clusters and associations throughout the world (be it natural or man-made), and the doctrine's misplaced logic of the blame game in which today's bad people are exonerated, and the historically oppressive group shall be held in contempt evolves. That means, on the one hand, the traditional identities such as the nation-state shall be diluted by flooding with non-Westerners who share little in common. And, on the other hand, the oppressed shall be given the platform, the identity, and the means, unwittingly or not, to demand and seek retribution for the supposed injustices.

Liberalism's assault on the traditional family structure, on the two genders, weakens the familial environment for responsible child growth. On another front, the weakening of the nation-state by multiculturalism, the weakening of the family structure and the creation over time of the feckless individual together contribute to the swift erosion – within the span of two to three generations from the time the tools of decay become mainstream – of Western values. Country, faith, family values, and service become anathema. Those who cherish them invite scorn. The intensity of decline only worsens over time.

The distinct values of the West characterize Western Civilization and within the West the culture and mores influenced by language, geography, and history that shape and bind together the inhabitants of a territory distinguish a Western nation that is organized politically under a sovereign state. The dilution of Western culture by historically non-Western peoples, who do not share western values or assimilate into western culture, shall constitute as a matter of definition an assault upon the West. That causes to the receding of western values, to the Western society in the Western domain, to the decline of Western Civilization, and of the Western idea.

The trend on the tradition front by weakening the borders and western values; on the economic front by the state control of the economy; and on the religion front by reducing the influence of faith in the newer generations by removing prayer from schools, by indoctrination in colleges and universities (staffed by the liberals) – to achieve the goals of "equality" and "justice" – amount to the fullest implementation of Modern Liberalism.

More importantly, the nexus between Liberalism's "one man, one vote" principle on the political front and opposition to the supposedly abstract nation-state and to the concept of national sovereignty on the tradition front means that liberals harbor strong internationalist tendencies. A Super World government – in the line of thought of the Worldwide Socialist movement of the late nineteenth and twentieth century – being able to centralize power and to eradicate every major and minor problem the planet is tainted with is a distant but worthy goal to the liberal. To the liberal, it is simply nonsensical to have the "one man; one vote" principle constrained to the national boundaries. This tendency in the minds of liberals may be referred to as Democratic Centralism. World Courts, World Leagues, World Forums, Global Cultural Exchange Programs are few of the ideal stratospheres of power for the liberal to aim at and built upon the like.

In the not so far away future, above all, from the economic, religion, and tradition dimension, the three-front assault on the

Western superstructure leads to two significant developments on the Western shore, in addition to causing the retreat of Western values by way of multiculturalism. First, the sacrifice of the liberal state– Liberalism's prior political stance; and second, the creation of room for encroachment of enemy from the outside– by way of its strict anti-war stance or from within– by way of multiculturalism outmaneuvering the local culture. Both developments only further fasten the inevitable weakening of the Western values and thereby the Western civilization.

That is Liberalism in the efforts to destroy traditional identities, weaken religion in private lives, subject economic activity to state control, provides room for state encroachment. And the opening to be taken advantage of by the enemy – be it state or non-state – that encroaches into the Western sphere rather stealthily.

Encroachment, accordingly, is to enter by gradual steps or by stealth into the possessions or rights of another, or, to advance beyond the usual or proper limits, as per Webster's dictionary.

The liberalization of society is duly promoted by the liberal intellectual through the institutions, supported by the liberal public, enacted and enforced by the state – with the pace of the process depending on all of the three. But the strength of the liberal public, just as a share of the voting population, is the determining factor of the pace of this process. That is so because, it is the most probable explanation as to why the infiltration of the key institutions, especially of the cultural megaphones of Academia, Arts, and the Media, has been carried out and duly guarded. In fact, that has been the standard denominator across the countries of the West that have been retreating from both outside and inside since the liberal march of the institutions.

Any organization or institution not chartered conservatively, that is the vision and mission of these institutions not designed to extract leeway in the adherence to the traditional morals and values become, both in the short-term and the long-term, a ripe target for takeover by the liberals, and in other cases where this may not be, the takeover is done simply by disregarding the rules, if needed. As to the cultural megaphones of Academia, Arts and the Media – infiltration by operatives, filtering out of non-liberals, etc. has been the case across the West.

To sum up: the relentless wave of the liberalization of society – a form of social engineering – yields to increasing encroachment by the state, which is not a priori but is caused by the liberals using the levels of the state to enforce an intended outcome. And also yields to the encroachment of state-enemy or non-state enemy, which is also not a priori, but an inevitable effect of the advantages sown in the field by a blindsided liberal society.

Encroaching State and Encroaching Enemy

To provide "equality" and "justice" for the supposed minority groups, the liberal elites backed by the liberal public petition the state to correct the wrongs, of social or economic, existing in the supposedly bad society, through legislation or by the ignorance of the existing laws. Thereby at specific instances, they consciously or unconsciously promulgate to the state to encroach on the rights of the people and to subvert the supreme laws of the land, never mind if the encroachment and subversion are from the bench, or the legislature, or the executive, or all the three. Every inch of equality bleeds that much degree of individual freedom.

Liberals and liberal elites march in unison in their efforts of subversion of the freedoms of the individual by petitioning the grievances to the state. Wherever the state, such as in the United States with the Republican ideals enshrined, is constitutionally prohibited from abridging certain freedoms – such as the freedom of speech, liberals themselves assume the force of the state in such a manner that society becomes steeped into deep and profound political correctness. Freedom of the press comes to be abused by subverting its tools for nefarious aims – propaganda and opinion delivered as daily news. Lying by omission, character assassination – few such tactics heavily borrowed from Soviet propaganda machine is put to work endlessly.

When a state enemy is at your doorstep, the liberal will tell you that it is to your benefit that the enemy is close enough that we can now monitor and make them feel captive, and then the liberal will soothe the naysayers that it is only for the greater good and world peace. When the enemy threatens to attack you, he will tell you that your response to the enemy with harsh rhetoric is reckless at best and unhinged at worst.

When a non-state enemy, inadvertently or not, is gradually creeping into the heartland, the liberal will tell you that your apprehension is baseless. He will not let go of you until he lists out all of the endless benefits they bring here, or the benefits you lose out if they are deported, or will scare you with the style of consequences it will result in if you dare suggest to stop them from entering anymore. The listing of the litany of benefits the country will have or will lose out is only the starter pack – as any naysayers who persist will then be damned; their speech suppressed, their views called out as extreme, their demands insane, and importantly, labeled with scaremongering names that they supposedly are.

The efforts in the silencing of the naysayers who oppose the erosion of traditional identities, religious freedom take the form of the policing of speech. Thus political correctness consumes society in trying to keep discourse in check within the accepted band of debate and discussion– a form of thought policing of the non-liberals, mostly, manned day-to-day, minute-by-minute, word-to-word, by the liberals for the liberals. Ordinarily by citing the dictate that freedom of speech does not entail freedom from the consequences of speech, the politically incorrect speaker is duly blackballed by the liberal thought-police. That was without realizing that both the speech code and the degree to which a specific speech attracts a particular consequence will change, as liberal intolerance for a specific band of speech evolves. That is what was considered safe speech by the liberals two decades ago may be deemed as hate speech today, notwithstanding the fact that the terms 'safe' and 'hate' cannot be harmonized with the behavior in question – speech – due to the nature of the action.

In the name of diversity, liberals encourage dilution of the nation states of the West with people migrating from non-Western regions. During the Age of Consolidation of Liberalism, therefore, the United States and the United Kingdom, and many other Western European countries have been flooded with migrants from all over the globe who do very little on their part to assimilate into the local culture. In fact, the day does not seem too far off when local people will be forced by liberals to assimilate into the cultures of the immigrant. Modern Liberalism has been a beacon of hope to carry out this task.

The uncomfortable consequences that begin to show up inevitably in society due to Operation Diversity are employed to the full-effect by the liberal into further eradication of the traditional society and the remnants if any of the nation-state. The signs of the West receding swiftly manifest in the form of increasingly frequent liberal hysteria or outcry sparked in the aftermath of a crisis in the eyes of the liberal. Thus calling for a permanent takedown of things such as those of monuments of founding fathers that have been part of the culture, the tradition, and the nation. And eventually of the people who were the heart and soul of the West.

All of the freedoms cherished and guarded until then by the people come under attack because the liberal demands for resolving the liberal-deemed crisis involves the sacrifice of the liberty of the people, the culture, and eventually the full nations of the West. The freedom to defend and secure oneself and his family from the scourge of lawlessness also comes under attack because the liberal goes so far as to claim that the freedom to defend oneself from harm's way is traditional, anachronistic, and offensive to others.

However, the permanent takedown of the things that have been part of the culture, the tradition, the nation, and the people is a process in the eradication that to the non-liberal mind appears to be deeply regressive in its method and its outcome. That is when everything that had been part of society comes under question and relentlessly attacked from every side, the only result that emerges out of those malignant attacks is the forceful redefinition of all things natural, cultural, and traditional. The process of liberalization of society thus is deeply "regressive," and it is anything but "progressive."

Thus, it soon becomes that Liberalism's unceasingly apparent contradiction in everyday life is the inevitable turn against its ideal of free speech.

In the Age of mass communication, pamphlets of the past had been overturned altogether by a few corporatist monopolies characterizing the Age of Monopolized communication platforms. In this Age, at the time of consolidation of Liberalism, the impulse to censor reflects what may be the insecurities of the society, or precisely of the liberal section of the society, to the looming crisis of confidence in Liberalism and the inevitable fight back that ensues against this mentally crippling doctrine.

The drive to censorship in the Age of Monopolized communication platforms, barring major intervention, does not recede and if anything, the degree of censorship becomes pervasive for the simple reason that there exists no reason not to do so, especially as the fight back intensifies.

Modern Liberalism and Fascism – A Shared Outlook

Fascism seeks ultimate state control of everything except for private property and private ownership of the big business that shall be regulated in the operations to the detail. Importantly it seeks the power and control of the Press and Academia. It engages in the suppression of free speech, vehemently opposing dissenting views. And it forces on the people the state-imposed doctrine, takes away the right to self-defense by seizing the arms from the people and advocates eugenics. Those have been the core features of Fascism, or in other words, that was the kind of social structure and society-state relationship observed in the countries that were called Fascist. What can be unambiguously inferred from such a state of affairs in those countries is the result of the loss of the freedom of the individual due to the monolithic, all-powerful state. Mussolini in his speech before the Chamber of Deputies on May 26, 1927 captured the Fascist philosophy "Everything in the State, and nothing outside the State, nothing against the State." It stands as a valid observation of the times.

Modern Liberalism, in the name of equality and justice to the supposed minority groups, seeks state-control of the crucial sectors of the economy, such as Healthcare and Education. It allows private ownership of the big business that shall be regulated in the operations to the detail, and the small business regulated until bankrupted, leaving only the big business. The liberal march through the institutions, seeking the control of the Press, and Academia, manifests in the liberal indoctrination of society. And wherever the state cannot it shall conceive along with the liberal public to suppress the freedom of speech, especially of the non-liberal type to guard the liberal doctrine. It shall together petition the duly obliging state to take away the right to self-defense by seizing the arms from the people, and shall stringently advocate and provide state-funding for abortion in the name of "family planning." If Modern Liberalism ushered in the kind of social structure and the society-state relationship that is recognized as such, what may unambiguously be inferred from such a state of affairs is the result in the loss of the freedoms of the individual due to the monolithic, all-powerful state. Again the observation "Everything in the State, and nothing outside the State, nothing against the State" stands.

Modern Liberalism is Fascism, coming in slowly and gradually from the back door. A check mark to detect whether an ideology has inherent totalitarian tendencies is by noticing its command on the society including the degree of reality such a society can glean; one should go beyond theory and verify in practice whether the ideology has warped reality, or in the midst of doing so, across the spectrum of life. In one form or another, explicitly or discreetly, one may find in the Western hemisphere the liberal doctrine taking a romantic place in Sports, movies, radio, drama, media, schools, colleges, the permanent state bureaucrat machinery, etc. Only those institutions specially geared for non-liberal politics may in the long-run escape being run over by Liberalism. If Soviet Communism had any lost siblings, to the busy mind now looking for it, Liberalism in the West would be a strong contender.

Fascism and Modern Liberalism in fact amount to a significant development on the idea of Communism in practice. Whereas Communism controlled everything and engaged in the execution of the task itself by taking ownership of everything, Fascism and Liberalism constricted to the control part leaving the job of execution to various private parties. That is why private property was never entirely abolished in the fascist regimes. It was easy for them to simply order what they wanted, whether it was a particular kind of ammunition, or a certain form of service, or a certain piece of propaganda dissemination. The state merely orders, and the private parties deliver. Herein lies the exact reason behind the kind of private-state structure that evolved in fascist regimes. Since Fascism as a matter of history had developed in capitalist countries, it was easy and smart for the fascist parties to simply build on and reorganize the existing executing infrastructure rather than trying to re-do. For them restructuring the infrastructure to have it turned subservient to their control and demand seemed to be practical, strategic and easy. Engaged in traditional capitalist countries, Modern Liberalism, likewise, has had been able to afford much comfort to not only bring into the state-control the culture apparatus but had the advantage of being able to do it stealthily. Fascism and Modern Liberalism are the creation of smart people who knew what they wanted at the time. That, in fact, may be the reason why Modern Liberalism, with its stealth and nimble movements, do not conjure an image of anything other than that of a faceless, pragmatic and innocuous political ideology.

If Fascism and Modern Liberalism share in the common desire for that flexible and smart structure that as stated already amounts to a solid upgrade on communism, the tactics adopted by the two starkly differ. Fascism in the European varieties destroyed the opposition to it by various cruel means; Modern Liberalism, on the contrary, has been a slow-walking squad masquerading its sinister motives and trying to rattle the opposition into panic while emboldening its grip on the subjects with niceties. That is Modern Liberalism is Fascism with a smiley face. Thus in the tactics, Modern Liberalism manifestly departs from Fascism, but the enduring visions of the two remain a common and shared interest. It is the envisioning and the eventual realization of the kind and the structure of the society-state relationship, and not the tactic by which to get there, that Modern Liberalism shares parallel with Fascism. And it is only in that sense that Modern Liberalism is Fascism and this emphasis and qualification remains in that matter.

If Classical Liberalism culminated in the fallout leading to the fast rise of Fascism from the front door, Modern Liberalism shapes into Fascism, only slowly, from the back door. But why is this the case and what is the internal mechanism that is causing this?

That is all the more not so surprising, even technically how this may be the case that why both Classical Liberalism and Modern Liberalism culminate, directly or indirectly, into Fascism and it is mightily clear from the economic standpoint and that which we'll turn first.

It is because the corrective measures in the aftermath of the devastation of society due to the fallout from Classical Liberalism and the failure of liberal politics, when quick adjustments to the few institutions concerning money, trade and finance sufficed for stabilization, the state instead had gone beyond what was necessary and had culminated in Fascism. Since then, wherever the state has made timely adjustments or benefited from special conditions (US and UK), and wherever the state returned to normalcy later on after the upheavals of the Second World War (France, Germany), the corrective measures resulted in the control of the economic sectors. That measures were advocated by and provided with the necessary ideals of Modern Liberalism, and those have been nothing but gradual steps in the direction to the same place that previously had been reached in one giant step by going beyond what was necessary for the name of the supposed corrective measure.

From social standpoint, the duly obliging state, in its efforts to provide "equality" and "justice" to minority groups, necessitates infringement of the freedoms of the people and therefore to the gradual state encroachment of society, reaching an outcome similar to the one enacted by going beyond what was necessary to contain the fallout from Classical Liberalism.

The Fascist regimes sacrificed the liberal state to achieve the purported ends on the economic and social front. In the modern times, the Liberal intellectuals and the liberal society to achieve the purported ends on the economic and social front are sacrificing the liberal state.

As said elsewhere, the power of Fascist regimes to transform the state considerably turned easy during the conditions of what may be called the permanent state of emergency in the country. In the US, Progressivism, the father of Modern Liberalism, also enjoyed emergency-like conditions during war times, just enough for the implementation of policies that allowed state expansion to unprecedented heights – a topic reviewed in Chapter Five.

The FDR and LBJ administrations, coming in after the unfolding of transformative events in the Great Depression and the assassination of President Kennedy, enjoyed what could be called semi-emergency or emergency-like conditions, thereby being able to legislate and execute policies of Modern Liberalism. The emergency conditions in the US in the aftermath of the September-eleven attacks had proved fit in the name of security to transform the state into surveillance state. It had afforded the conditions to briskly accept, fund and enact a massive surveillance super infrastructure able to spy on citizens to be later used to unmask if needed the names of political enemies caught up in the collection of foreign intelligence. Surely the East German communist government would not have been disappointed.

All state laws, rules and regulations are nothing but a dictum governing the behavior of subject-individual. Even the ultimate purpose serving the existence of government is for it to regulate behavior of individuals to one end. All such dicta are singular, blanket, approved behavior for to be adhered by everyone. The more those dictates are, the more the individual's freedom of choice will be limited. The farther those dictates reach, the smaller the individual's freedom to shape his destiny. The wider those dictates reach, all the way to speech, self-defense and work, the smaller will be the band of acceptable behavior, prohibiting the individual to live a free life. The more a society wants to have all individuals act in one specific way, it becomes less free and the state more tyrannical. The path toward that territory may arrive at different times, under different banner-names, and in different ways, the behavior of the individual, of which the state tries to regulate, is limited in the few important dimensions – such as thought and speech, association, work etc. Whether the ideology that comes to influence state-action may be popularly called A or B, but the regulation restricting the individual to pick blue only when there exist dozen other choice of colors inevitably suppresses freedom.

Modern Liberalism enables liberal elites and liberal politicians to jump on the bandwagon to grab and centralize more and more power from the people in return for promises to organize society in a more equal and just fashion. The visions of Republicanism's power to the people and Liberalism's power to the state couldn't have been further apart.

Chapter Eight
Republicanism to Liberalism in the United States

Attacks on the Constitution and the Bill of Rights

T he powers of Congress have been enumerated explicitly in the US Constitution, limiting by design the ever-expanding tentacles of power grab by the powerful. Thus, the enforcement of laws limited to this by the executive and the judiciary meant limited federal governance.

The republican form of government underscores the concept of empowering the federal or central government with limited powers, while the rest of the powers not vested with the state government reside solely in the individual. A transition from republican ideals to liberal ideals of government had effectively reversed this power structure in the US, making the federal government the single biggest monolithic, all-powerful force.

In the United States, during the first and second decade of the twentieth century, as the Age of Industrial Revolution ended and the Age of Modernization began, the state had been transformed from one of laissez-faire to interventionist. The transformation of the state could not have been possible without the abandonment of the ideals of Republicanism of the founding fathers enumerated by them in the original Constitution and the Bill of Rights in favor of the ideals of twentieth century Liberalism. The instituting of constitutional amendments had critically enabled that transformation. And more importantly, to that effect there began a subversion of the founding document to the extent possible by the US Supreme Court and the Executive branch.

The Sixteenth amendment to the Constitution, ratified in February 1913, has given Congress the right to lay and collect taxes on all kinds of income. The Federal Reserve Act, signed into law by the Progressive President Woodrow Wilson in December 1913, established the Federal Reserve System, giving it the authority to issue notes as legal tender, mandating it to respond to the stresses of the banking system efficiently and to create a stable financial system. The original 1913 Act has been amended numerous times since then, expanding the activities of the Fed considerably. The Fed had come to control the monetary policy of the United States; it was later mandated to effectively promote the goals of maximum employment, stable prices, and moderate long-term interests. Even though the President appoints Board members of the Federal Reserve System, the startling lack of accountability of any kind on the institution does not comport with the principles enshrined in the Constitution.

Even as eager economists like to justify the mandated powers of the Fed by emphasizing that the Fed requires autonomy from the whims of popular government, that reasoning, however, misses the point. The notion of accountability that just as much applies to any other public authority and being central to the whole idea of government in the first place is crucially absent. The peculiar structure of the Fed workings becomes plain during such transformative events of the recent times. The Fed's role in the financial crisis and the recession that followed is a case in point. In the aftermath of the crisis, no bureaucrat, no banker, no executive was prosecuted, as there just never existed a notion of accountability in regards to autonomous entities, or of justice under the rule of law for criminal activities.

Today the change of ideals in the US manifests in numerous ways. The Republican ideals of limited government, guaranteeing the most freedoms to the citizen, and the rule of law have now during the twenty-first century been turned upside down. Big bureaucratic government; the first amendment prohibiting the state from abridging the freedom of speech has been sanctimoniously abridged on behalf of the state through political correctness enforced by liberal thought-police; the second amendment of the right to keep and bear arms had come to stand on a razor edge margin in the US Supreme Court, and the increasing sight of the rule of lawlessness and the subversion of the law.

This transformation of the ideals from Republicanism to Liberalism, and hence the subversion of the Constitution, manifests in the radical remaking of the three branches of the federal government, the dilution of the separation of powers, partly leading to and partly because of radical reinterpretation of the Constitution by all three branches, primarily by the US Supreme Court, and the increasing power-grab of the federal government from the states, partly as a result of Constitutional amendments ratified after the Civil War, and also due to 1913 Constitutional amendment giving the people the right to elect Senators directly instead of state legislatures – a move that eroded the states' sovereign representation in one chamber of the Bicameral Legislature.

Principally, the pace and extent of transformation paralleled the rise and consolidation of Liberalism during the twentieth century; that is, the liberal transformation of the public and civil society, including the Media, the Arts and the Academia had enabled and greased the change.

Importantly, the ideals of limited government came to be diluted throughout the twentieth century. In the case of the executive branch, the role of the President as enumerated in the Constitution primarily comes down to being the top executive of the federal government. He shall have appointment powers but limited by the Senate's role of advice and consent and shall faithfully enforce the laws of the land. He checks the Legislature with the power to sign or veto Bills but limited by the power of Congress to override the veto. And additionally, being the head of state with war-making and treaty-making power, but only again limited by the Senate's role of giving authorization and consent respectively. Lastly, the President is conferred with the power of pardon.

What transpired during the twentieth century has been a radical departure from the originally vested powers, as the President had come to deploy military force unilaterally, ignoring the War Powers Resolution. The President had now come to take the role of Chief Legislator when no such duty is even hinted in the Constitution. As it stands, all legislative powers are vested in Congress. There has been, even more, dilution of separation of powers as the executive branch of the federal government took over the role of Congress by assuming the role of enacting regulations by unelected bureaucrats.

The Judiciary began to interpret the laws enacted by Congress liberally, thereby rewriting the laws from the bench, together undermining the will of the people as reflected in specific laws passed by the Congress, which among the three had historically had the most sizable non-liberal brain trust constituted in the members.

The consolidation of Liberalism can also be discerned in the ever-declining role and scope of non-governmental institutions that are primarily traditional in character and existence, such as churches, voluntary associations and organizations in society, and the proportionate rise of the role of the state in all matters of the society. The state control of the lives of people, as noted previously, by the advocacy of Liberalism since the twentieth century but especially since the Age of Liberal consolidation, has been a clear turn on the earlier ideals it had advocated, namely, freedom and liberty.

During the twentieth century, attempts to remodel the society meant employment of a different set of ideals on the part of the doctrine to service favorable outcome, namely "equality" and "justice." The state was then reconstructed to transform the society by the active and vigorous encroachment of those same freedoms of the individual, and in addition to the subversion of anything in its path, be it the Constitution or the Bill of Rights. Underpinning this giant transformation was the steadfast adherence to the idea among the liberal elite that the society's interests should trump the freedom of the individual.

That is why it is not hard to see why the US Constitution, since the turn of the twentieth century, had come to be interpreted among the influential sections of the society as a living document. That has therefore paved for the Constitution to be read according to the times and not according to the original meaning, which in practice as a result had enabled a great many liberal Judges to advance the cause of progressive transformation of society. In one way, Liberal antagonism toward the Constitution stems from it being a creature of the past that has to be shredded away to enact one suitable for the present times and wishes.

Attacks on Life, Liberty and the Pursuit of Happiness

Since the early twentieth century, the society had gradually been taken over by Liberal creed, first among the intellectuals and then among the public. The contradictions that are inherent in it, therefore, manifest increasingly in the real world. Implementation of policies drawn from an endless swell of liberal ideals of "equality" and "justice" in varied aspects of social life is possible, with the possibility being roughly proportionate to the extent of society taken into the liberal fold means over time the increasing manifestation of liberal contradictions. In other words, the highest level of liberal inconsistencies become apparent when significant portions of society, especially of the intellectual variety, is consumed by it. Thus, it may be stated unequivocally that when Liberal creed's top ideals, the freedom of speech, comes under attack from Liberals themselves – hence the inherent contradiction – it is so because the Liberal creed itself has come under attack.

The Age of Late Electronics Revolution's gift of monopolized communication platforms meant the liberals that staff the monopolies duly oblige the demands by liberals for censorship and suppression of speech deemed extreme by them. Liberals, that which undoubtedly qualifies as an act of the suppression of speech, run through the liberal converter to interpret the speech in question as a violation of the encoded corporate code of conduct, or the code of usage.

The Fourth Amendment to the Constitution guarantees people the right to privacy. It says the right of the people to be secure in their persons, houses, papers, and effects, against unreasonable searches and seizures shall not be violated, and no Warrants shall be issued, except upon probable cause, supported by Oath or affirmation, and particularly describing the place to be searched, and the persons or things to be seized. The gift of a monopolized communication platform to violate this right, and henceforth the usurpation of power has been underway for some time – the surveillance state had become a permanent thing of the federal government. Mussolini who touted the mantra "Everything in the State, and nothing outside the State, nothing against the State" would probably not speak ill of this development.

The case of just how much surveillance is being carried out by the state is a topic unto itself. But those harboring doubts as to the legitimacy of the existence of a permanent surveillance apparatus of online activity shall find no comfort to comprehend that the contemporary state was remodeled to reflect modern liberalism's thinking. The state in the twentieth century was transformed to do anything and should get away with anything so long as it has been deemed good and serves the interests of the society by them. That, therefore, the state inevitable engages the mass communication platforms to that effect if it hadn't yet is a no-brainer.

In the Age of Consolidation of Liberalism, according to the liberals, the closing in of state enemy, or the creeping in of non-state enemy into the heartland of the country is only for the greater good; anybody who dares voice an opinion that it is not the case welcomes swift attacks; the naysayers are marginalized and in the Age of monopolized communication, their speech promptly suppressed, while the protectionist state encroaches on other freedoms of the people, such as the right to keep and bear arms that come handy for defense against an enemy.

The liberal elite in the Age of Liberalism while duly enabling the above cause looks forward to and helps make the liberal dream come true. First, the protectionist state protects wealth being accumulated in absurd concentrations by the elite, duly enforced by rigging the system in the name of free markets, and co-opts with the liberal society to tear down traditional identities including gender, family and marriage, religion and, most important to the elite, the nation-state. Secondly, the state strives to outlaw the freedoms of the individual to speech and self-defense in the name of rights of others that in fact amount to super-privileges. And third, the state promotes and pays for the cause of abortion-on-demand in the name of women's rights, in addition to shortchanging the lives of people by marginalizing them and playing down the threat posed by the encroaching enemy in the name of equality and justice. Thus the state originally constituted to protect life, liberty and the pursuit of happiness have then been transformed to one that strives to deprive the individual all of the three in the reverse order of the points laid out. That is a move toward the pursuit of the liberal dream world wherein an identity-less, property-deprived, and freedoms-curtailed, and life-marginalized person becomes just another number in the collective world entity. An entity that is devoid of any groups, except for the liberal elite who constitute the world government that governs and strives for the motto "all men are equal, but some men are more equal than others."

Chapter Nine

The Rescuing of the West

Liberalism and its Discontents

Classical Liberalism guaranteed freedom and liberty including the freedom of choice with having the Self-regulating market (state intervention being absent). But the system rendered the individual to an unbearable ordeal and delivered severe social costs. That effectively resulted in the grievances that going unresolved had culminated into the front door of Fascism that purported to solve all the consequences in a big step, but in return took away all of the freedoms in one large bite.

Modern Liberalism guaranteed equality and justice, and it determined therefore to eradicate all the associations, social identities, and economic inequities that existed in the society. That had come to be executed by the liberals petitioning the state to resolve the grievances all in small steps, but the state in return took away all of the freedoms in small bites. The state has been going unstopped in time to slowly culminate in Fascism from the back door.

Referring to the state at this development as "Big Government" is just a colloquial expression. Both consequential forces led to the ever-growing power of the state. To quote Mussolini, "Everything in the State, and nothing outside the State, nothing against the State" – accordingly the state manifests itself inside across all spheres of life, tangible or intangible, including thought and speech. Wherever there are robust checks against tyrannical forces, as in the United States – codified in the Constitution and the Bill of Rights, the road in the slow culmination into the backdoor of Fascism inevitably involves subversion and ignorance of the law. That inevitably leads to the undermining of the rule of law paving way to Anarchy.

In the United States, during the Age of Consolidation of Liberalism, attacks on the First Amendment that prohibits the state from abridging the freedom of speech, on the Second Amendment, prohibiting the state from infringing the right of the people to keep and bear arms, therefore, may be interpreted to be the efforts towards decimating the last barriers to reaching the liberal dream world.

Therefore, we have come full circle wherein the American Bill of Rights guaranteeing the freedom of speech and the right of the people to keep and bear arms is threatened by the actions of the people who subscribe to the doctrine of Liberalism – the political philosophy supposedly underlying the American project. To historians, Republicanism (or whatever term that may be assigned to the philosophy of the American founding fathers) and Classical Liberalism did not appear distinct. As much the philosophy of John Locke influenced the American founding fathers, the doctrine of Liberalism had been shaped no less. That is why today the people in the United States who believe in the ideals that have been characterized as republicanism in this book identify themselves as classical liberals– a throwback to nineteenth century limited government.

United Kingdom Does not exist in the Minds of Liberals

Liberals in the United States and the United Kingdom actively look to the day the multicultural dream is fulfilled and the nation-state is diluted. In the culmination of the receding of the nation-states across the West, the liberals and their associates such as immigrants who previously had never belonged to the West corrupt the system and the way of life. The mechanisms employed by them to this effect, unsurprisingly, involve the abuse of rights and freedoms guaranteed in those Western countries, and gradually, the corruption of the governing polity itself. By keeping this point in mind, the intensity with which the destructive tendencies set in motion, which snowball in the process and culminate in the full-scale receding of the West, depends on the swiftness with which the liberals and their associates attain a simple majority to take over the governing polity for good.

The efforts to preserve the nation-states in the West, by severing ties with supranational polities such as the European Union, unsurprisingly witness attacks from all sides. Liberal elites, in such cases as Great Britain, claim that there never existed a nation-state of Great Britain; that there was the British Union, British Empire and Britain as a unit of European Union. But this is a subtle manipulation of words, meaning, and history. Undoubtedly, in the distant past, there was a nation of England that entered into union with its neighbors on the island and with another island, Ireland, situated in the Western shores. But that is beside the point of contention. There indeed never was a Great Britain in theory in the recent past – just the British Empire. But the usage of the concept of Empire to identify the polity governing the people of Great Britain is a neat trick in that if it weren't the case, there would never have existed a civilization called the West. There is the West, and there is everything else. It is in the character of the West, in the language, religion, custom, tradition, values, morals that there had evolved an idea called the West, differentiating itself from everything else.

For the West to exist, there needs to be a different place from which the West can carve itself out to be known, in the full amalgam and display of its character, as Western civilization. If that was not the case, the Age of Industrial Revolution might never have happened, or if it did, it would encompass regions beyond – for the purposes and with no other name that comes to mind we reserve to call the region – the West. In the case of Great Britain, apparently to the cynics the existence of British flag – during and after the Empire enterprise – does not pass for national symbol of affirmation of common identity and shared destiny.

Thus, by recognition of Western civilization differentiating itself from others, the nation of Great Britain had always existed within the greater idea of the Empire itself – as the flag of Great Britain attests. That whole notion of Great Britain as a nation is in fact very simple. The idea is simple enough that a regular British citizen, lacking breadth and depth in historical knowledge that enamors the liberal elite who befall into spewing meaningless manipulative distorted talking points, understand quite sharply. At least clear enough to envision a British nation-state and to go vote to exit the Union for its realization in practice.

United States – Free Speech & the Electoral College

The American founding fathers devised the Electoral College to avoid the tyranny of the simple majority– part and parcel of having textbook democracy, which they disliked. They construed textbook democracy to be nothing more than rule by an elected mob, free to reign-in anybody they disliked. It serves to recall that the liberals and their associates milk the existing institutions to its fullest extent including the democratic system as well. In the Age of Consolidation of Liberalism, the Electoral College in the United States, to some extent and some degree, stretches the time upon when the attaining of simple majority becomes feasible. Additionally, the liberal-dominated cultural megaphones, especially Media, but even the other two at times, strive to exhibit the mantle of their liberal leadership in the society, and as the guardians and purveyors of the doctrine of Liberalism, they duly marginalize those who intend to stop the march to the dream world. Censorship of speech in the Age of monopolized communication platforms, in combination with the abuse of the Press, becomes a daunting task to counter the forces of Liberal hysteria, as a result.

In this Age, censorship of speech and the rising use of other subtler weapons to destroy the opposition is something that the liberals, especially the liberal press, deploy to the fullest effect. In that respect indoctrination, manipulation, distortion, and other social and language engineering are few such mechanisms employed to this effect by the press. As an example, it has surprisingly gone unnoticed over a few decades now, to my knowledge, that these two words "controversial" and "conspiracy" as widely understood today, at the least in the political landscape, are a result of radical redefinition. The Press has effectively 'controversialized' the word controversy and 'conspiratorialized' the word conspiracy and has indoctrinated the radical redefinitions to the public at large.

Webster defines "controversy" as "a discussion marked especially by the expression of opposing views" and conspiracy as [is] "to join in a secret agreement to do an unlawful or wrongful act or an act, which becomes unlawful as a result of the secret agreement" or "to act in harmony toward a common end."

Accordingly, the word "controversy" in such expressions as "controversial views of the man," or "a controversial figure" shall mean the man or the figure holds opposing views and brings a radically different opinion to the table, as compared to the opinion of a counterpart. Of what was a harmonious and innocuous description of a person, the word "controversy" has then been sent to the liberal engineering laboratory to be redefined. And subsequently post indoctrination it came to be understood to mean something extreme, fishy, troubling, and even dangerous. The word "controversy" as per the original Webster meaning has a very solid, useful, and essential meaning and role to it. It serves to imply that the person next to you disagrees with you while saying nothing about the nature of the opposite views at all.

In the same vein, the word "conspiring" that just as the word "dangerous" is highly innocuous and essential to intelligent communication. But it had been engineered to become bloated thanks to the liberal indoctrination to mean that it is extreme, incorrect, unreal, debunked, or even literal insane, henceforth to suggest the person is not credible. Expressions such as "this person is a conspiracy theorist" or "this man believes in conspiracies" function well to that effect. The word "conspiring" as per the original Webster definition implies nothing more than that there is another explanation of the plot or of the publicly transpired events, not known publicly. Simply, it means there is another up-to-now unknown explanation, aside from the mainstream explanation, to the publicly transpired events. What had that term been turned into? That there is one explanation, and one that is consented and mainstream; and that there is no other explanation. Anybody who pushes a different one, whether it may turn to be correct or incorrect, is insane, as per the engineered definition that is "conspiracy."

Complicating the matters, in this case, is the real existence of certain explanations that may be called conspiracy theories, as per the engineered definition. But in many cases, there may exist second explanation, which after a full investigation turns out to be the correct explanation. That secondary explanation may supersede the mainstream version in the credibility as evidence rolls in. The problem arises when conflating the two: the first case, the explanation that is a conspiracy theory, as per the engineered definition, and in the other case, the explanation that is second to the mainstream ending up valid and credible.

The terms "Conspiracy" and "Controversy" are critical to the narrative-making business. In the Age of the liberal control of the cultural megaphones, shaping favorable narrative therefore takes utmost importance. Henceforth, Modern Liberalism on all of its active fronts – economic, religion, and tradition – employs language engineering of this sort to the fullest effect. Many terms such as these take refugee in contrived meaning, undergo surreptitious transformation, and attract irreconcilable interpretation.

Likewise, in this day and age, progressivism in practice is actually regressive; unaffordable healthcare is packaged as the Affordable Care Act; fascists come as antifascists; anti-religious anti-tradition attitude brings out the open-minded side; freedom of religion is discriminatory; violence, where that fits the narrative, is peaceful, speech that is disliked is hateful; right to self-defense and border defense is racism and bigotry; proclaiming to protect those rights reflects conduct that is hateful and divisive; smearing passes for due process; mob (media) judgment passes for justice; drive-by shot passes for objective news; willful blindness and lying by omission is presented as objective journalism; narcissism, victim-hood, and female-dominance is repackaged as feminism (the third wave variety); demonizing men is fine to oppose patriarchy; motherhood becomes unpalatable, fatherhood means too much responsibility.

As the liberal attempts to provide "equality" and "justice" for the minority groups by petitioning the state that is constituted to a large extent by the liberal elite eager to subvert or undermine the law, it begins to infringe on the rights and freedoms of the people. The burden to defend freedoms, including the freedom of speech, therefore falls on those desired to protect and conserve them. As may be the case in the Age of Consolidation of Liberalism, the list of things to conserve keeps expanding.

As already stated, it may be roughly approximated that in the Age of Consolidation of Liberalism, an increasing share of each of new generation fell into the liberal fold. Thus, the fight back against Liberalism rests in on that old generation that is big enough, which in the US is the baby boomer, and living in the age when the last remaining vest of tools, chiefly the valuable tool of free speech that has long been under attack, are still around.

In practice, the size of the old generation may not be enough to provide dominant force in the fight back in those countries with textbook style democracy, since the younger generations – which constitute an increasingly higher share of liberals – could easily negate and dilute the votes of older generations by counter-voting them. But in practice, the United States is very much further away from being a textbook style democracy; it is a constitutional republic defined by a Constitutionally enforced Electoral College and the Bill of Rights designed to do away with the tyranny of the majority such as this one.

Therefore, against the encroaching state and the encroaching enemy, both promoted and reconciled to us by Liberalism; and amidst the bullying by the liberal institutions including the Media, Arts and Academia, the liberal non-profits; the tools left to defend the ideals of Republicanism essentially come down to the few remnants. They are free speech and the Electoral College system that is the single door to power before Liberalism abandons and revolts against both of them, as it inevitably will, given the insurmountable reactionary forces it shall duly encounter.

Chapter Ten

The Errors of Enlightenment – Part One

Liberalism and the Form of Government

The philosophical distinction between the two doctrines Republicanism and Liberalism manifestly comes to light in their views on the nature of social contract that so much exemplifies the form of government instituted based on either of them. Therefore a brief exploration into the contract between the individual and the state of the two products of the enlightenment is necessary. At this level, a stark difference between the two stands out over the question of the legitimacy of the authority of the state. Republicanism believes in the concept that the people are sovereign, whereas Liberalism holds that the sovereignty resides essentially in the nation and that nobody, no individual, can exercise authority that does not proceed from it in plain terms and that which is expressed in universal suffrage.

Whereas Republicanism identifies the individual as sovereign, endowed with certain inalienable freedoms bestowed by their Creator, Liberalism necessarily contradicts this by claiming that sovereignty resides in the collective entity, such as the nation, and therefore the state should exercise the rule by the general will of the people. The idea of the "general will" reinforces the notion that the individual couldn't be free, except as part of the collective group and that all the rights endowed to the individual originate, if there is any importance laid in the indication of the source of the rights, from here – the collective. More like, Liberalism believes the rights come from the government.

How does this distinction affect the governance in practice? An excellent place to begin is by stating what Liberalism wants to do in the mission as believed and advocated by the doctrine. Liberalism essentially holds that the good society can be achieved and is a step away by following through on the mass education programs and the legislation of the good institutions (while getting rid of the bad ones). But what is implicitly emphasized in this form of governance is that the freedom of the individual, whose source relegated to the collective in the first place, shall be sacrificed in the unceasing quest to model the good society without the permission of the individual.

But what else is not underscored, explicitly or implicitly at the philosophical level or at the level of the ideals held by it dearly is that the good society is a myth. There is no good society ever; at least with the given that the society is blessed with a liberal state, there is a society, and that is that. Liberalism's incorrect view of the nature of Man grossly distorts the model of society it wants to create. In fact, we may be able to construe here an abstract model of that society by touching on all of the four dimensions of the doctrine of Liberalism and the two core axioms it holds. The progressively good-natured man (human nature) values reason (attained from education). The man employs it to the fullest extent (reason taking the central place) in all manners and types of individual and social activities, without the constraint of ignorance, dogma, custom, tradition, and authority (anti-religion and anti-tradition stance). He makes use to the fullest extent of the rights and freedoms (human rights) including his right to cast the one vote guaranteed from the principle of equal universal suffrage (textbook democracy) to enact the good institutions. And he acts in the rationally self-interested manner (economic laissez-faire) to provide for the self, and on the whole, strives to change and transform the society into good society.

The French Revolution – and the First Revolutionary Liberals

To this day a crude misunderstanding of the kind of ideas that influenced the revolutionaries on both sides of the Atlantic in the latter part of the eighteenth century leaves many in confusion. And therefore it is necessary to resolve the issue at once here. It may appear that both Republicanism and Liberalism – the latter in the Classical form – influenced the movements and revolutions that transformed the state into the liberal state. But the philosophical distinctions between the two long remain even as many of the precepts held by both appear near identical, and therefore both seem the same. That is, one may be mistaken, as many liberal historians often are, especially in the twentieth century, that the original ideals of United States are the ideals of Liberalism; however, it is grossly incorrect. As long as the founding documents hold that there are certain inalienable rights of the individual, including the right to life, and also that the people are sovereign, this form of social contract as believed by the American founding fathers is the doctrine of Republicanism (the ideals held together under that term). Liberalism is entirely different as was evident at places that touched on the subject of the distinction between the two.

Liberalism, as it was, influenced the French Revolution. The American founding fathers were influenced by the writings of Enlightenment indeed. But guided by the experiences of life and faith they were wise enough to reject the illusions on human nature and the utopia of the good society. That brings us to the idea of certain egregious errors of the enlightenment philosopher, and about which we will discuss soon.

In the long march of the liberal dream to model and achieve the good society, guided by reason alone, there unfolds the transformation in which the state using the means of the general will of the people encroaches and violates the freedoms of the individual, leading in brief time to tyranny. This line of thinking sums up the logic and spirit behind the way in which French Revolution unfolded.

Whereas the Declaration of Independence, the American Revolutionary War, and the US Constitution and Bill of Rights revealed the ideals of Republicanism and espoused, in practice, by the wise men guiding the nation to freedom and independence by waging a just war against the tyrannical King. In the French Revolution the mob stormed the Bastille, in the National Assembly declared the Rights of Man and of the Citizen that held in the Article One that men are born free and remain free and equal in rights; in the Article Two that the aim of every political association is the preservation of the natural and imprescriptible rights of man and that these rights are liberty, property, security, and resistance to oppression; but also held in the Article Three that the source of all sovereignty resides essentially in the nation, and no body, no individual can exercise authority that does not proceed from it in plain terms; and in Article Four, to paraphrase, that the liberty of men has no limits except those that secure the enjoyment of these same rights to others and these limits are determined only by the law, and in the Article six that the law is the expression of the general will.

Thus the revolutionary document, in essence, proclaimed to guarantee all kinds of freedoms to the man in the First and Second Articles, then laid down where the sovereignty resides in the Third Article, which was not in the individual but the collective. And later it noted that only law could determine the limits to these freedoms guaranteed a while ago in the Articles One and Two, and declared in the Sixth Article that the general will is the law. That much was enough for the revolutionary mob to violate the guaranteed freedoms in the name of the general will; and under the threat of the guillotine to proceed beheading those who were considered by the mob the enemies of the

Revolution. Thus bringing in a short time the September massacres, the de-Christianization campaign, the beheading of Louis XVI, the beheading of Marie Antoinette, the Reign of Terror, and after a brief intervention the rule of the Directory, and then the military dictatorship.

The beheadings and the assassinations were daily spectacles in the four years of the Revolution. Death was demanded to traitors, spies, moderates, and dissenters, as decreed under the general will and exercised by the mob sitting on the ironically named *Committee of Public Safety* that was dominated by the Convention leader Maximilian Robespierre. As it was the case, all of those who disagreed with the Convention were put under the razor blade of the guillotine. Even the revolutionaries themselves being a part of the mob, including Robespierre himself and his followers, having been decreed by the ruling mob in July 1794 were sent to the guillotine one by one, thereby bringing to an end the Reign of Terror and to the takeover of power by the French Directory from the hands of the Committee.

That slew of excesses of the Revolution had made a mockery of the intent written at the beginning of the document and of the reasons for setting forth a solemn declaration like the scared rights of man. The document which held that ignorance, forgetfulness, or contempt of the rights of man are the sole causes of public miseries and the corruption of governments was forgotten sooner than imagined.

Ever since, the French Revolution's gift of the "general will" found home in twentieth century dictators who resorted to proclaiming that they were acting according to that will, never mind the ruthlessness in the exercise of it in practice. That notwithstanding of the fact that the guillotine of the French Revolution itself served as a model for these dictators for what to do after seizing power, or even to consolidate the existing power.

Notably, even more than a century after the French Revolution, the Russian revolutionaries in St. Petersburg saw it as a model to replicate. And the revolutionaries most passionately did, including the stage of beheading or assassinating the Monarchs.

More specifically, the French Revolution's underlying theses, laid down in those articles of the declaration, served as wellspring to a number of ideologies that came later on in the name of Socialism, Communism, Progressivism, Fascism, National Socialism, Technocracy etc. that produced these dictators, and whose edicts understood the importance of the general will as a means to achieving the utopian dream of the good society, and a task the ideologies strongly held that only the experts were well equipped to accomplish.

It is not a coincidence that the governance in the United States since the turn of the twentieth century, transformed by Progressivism, gave into a type of what can be called the rule by the elite. The march to utopia is laid out not by the public, at least not at first and only after being lured into the trap, but by the elite. Lenin, who along with a small mob, seized the Halls of Power; destroyed the opposition; laid down the road to utopia or the good society; is a prime example of what deranged intellectuals resort to for realizing their utopian dream, never mind the extermination of the opposition to their supposed general will. George Orwell's *Animal Farm* resembles not only Communism but also all the derivative ideologies that hold the general will as the principal tool; it is just that the ideologies differ in the flavor. Crucially the origin of the differences among them can be traced to the region and the pre-existing socio-political order. Nonetheless, they all display the totalitarian instincts that never fade away.

The enemy on the road to achieving the supposed good society is the free society. The longstanding observation is true – the road to tyranny is paved with good intentions.

Enlightenment's Obsession with Reason

The Age of Enlightenment created a political philosophy that had come to be called Liberalism, which for all its complexities had the underlying sediment proposing governance and social organization based exclusively on reason. Notwithstanding the leaps of progress the enlightenment thinkers had made, their excesses in the matters of human nature, socio-economic structure, and their attitude toward religion that bordered on rejecting the role of God had the unexpected effect of producing the brutalities the World has seen since then. The anti-religion stance in the spheres of life and governance was even before the advent of the Age of post-Darwin.

Jean-Jacques Rousseau, the intellectual father of the French Revolution, saw the state as the vessel to implement the "general-will." The bloody totalitarian dictatorships have drawn inspiration from Rousseau and the French Revolution. Rousseau's idea of the general will, exercised by a few select individuals, gave the world the many murderous dictators and room for their genocidal aims. With an absurd notion of human nature, many blanket programs have been conceived by a select group of elites and imposed inflexibly on the people to create the perfect society. That was an idea of governance practiced without a doubt to this day by the liberal elites supported by the liberals, drawing inspiration from and resting proudly on the shoulders of the legacy of the French Revolution and the doctrine of Liberalism.

Touched upon briefly elsewhere, the Enlightenment's obsession with reason naturally extended to religion. The theorists reasoned that everything, including religion, should be subservient to reason. But the role of reason in the affairs of governance becomes manifestly clear. The enlightened state instituted on reason empowered with the mission to carry out the "general will" therefore chooses to make religion subservient to the state. Or if necessary, just as the French Revolutionaries did, it prefers to discard the Church and make the state the new religion for mass worship. Inspired by Rousseau's writings on civic religion that held the view that the state should impose from the top down a universal code of religious beliefs, the French revolutionaries began the campaign of de-Christianization. They sought to erase Christianity and replace it with a religion of the state. The new universal religion of the enlightened state, the Cult of Reason, was an attempt to remake the remnants of the Church subservient to the state.

As Michael Kennedy notes in his book *The Jacobin Clubs in the French Revolution*, having disbanded the religion of Roman Catholicism, the French revolutionaries forced the Catholic priests to stand before the revolutionary clubs to take oaths to the newly instituted atheistic religion of France "The Cult of Reason." Twenty thousand priests took the oaths, but about the same number fled the country; ex-priests began to denounce their faith publicly, swearing they had never believed it. The revolutionaries decimated church art and statues; shredded sacred books; stole the gold and silver held by the churches as they deemed it was an insult to reason. And they turned the churches spared from destruction into homes of the revolutionary clubs. Church bells, thought to be a relic of fanaticism, were forbidden from being rung and were sometimes forcibly removed and melted down for armaments. The worship of reason kicked off with rituals held akin to pagan religions, with parades, dances, public burnings of the symbols of nobility. In one such instance of pagan rituals held in November 1793, the Notre Dame Cathedral was renamed "Temple of Reason," with the words "To Philosophy" carved into the façade, its crucifixes and other religious insignia stripped, the altar was engraved with the 'Altar of Reason."

If "reason" alone had to guide the affairs of the man and the society, then it is only reasonable to ask the question the German philosopher Immanuel Kant (1724 – 1804) famously raised, which may be summed up in the phrase "the limits of reason." Kant shattered the Age's romantic view toward reason and its supremacy. In his *Critique of Pure Reason* (1781) Kant theorized that human's perception of the world is severely dented by, or to state another way, is limited to the extent of the reach of, man's senses.

Chapter Eleven

The Errors of Enlightenment – Part Two

Adam Smith's Monstrous Theories

The Enlightenment's most famous philosopher-thinker, Adam Smith had conceived in his acclaimed 1776 magnum opus *The Wealth of Nations* the notion that the market comprised of self-interested individuals when left to its own devices can regulate itself under the rubric of the so-called invisible hand of the market. Because the state-intervened, universal-monopoly-tempered mercantile system was grossly inefficient, the Self-regulating market, Smith objectified, was the best recourse to pursuing the greatest good; that is, in the technical terms developed later on, it supposes the Self-regulating market yields Pareto optimal outcomes.

A great many thinkers have since then been deceived by this simplistic notion explaining the operations of markets, including Smith himself who appears to have stylized his invisible hand metaphor based on the prior, unintelligible poem by Bernard Mandeville in *The Fable of the Bees* (1714).

It has often been remarked that criticisms of *The Wealth of Nations* promptly disappear after a more rigorous and thorough understanding of Smith's thinking laid out in his prior book *The Theory of Moral Sentiments* (1759). But notwithstanding the wisdom in that work, there are well-placed, informed counter-points to Smith's erroneous contentions that have been taken as a given for more than two centuries now, and that which underlay the economic front of the doctrine of Classical Liberalism.

Adam Smith's economic system, as construed from his writings, shapes into a grand, capital-less, debt-free, labor-free, land-absent, technology-free, and uncertainty-less goods exchange system. And within this system, the hardworking pin factory owners, bakers, butchers, brewers, come together every day, or once a week, at a certain place to exchange each other's production based upon the needs and wants. A coin denominator that just happened to exist greases the exchange system of trading the produce of one another.

Apparently, in this system, the production of goods had already taken place in the background. It is sort of given into the system. The technology-less products such as meat and bread are produced, it is implicit in the argument, using the existing capital, by sole-owner-cum-laborer such as the butcher, the baker, who all bring in their surplus to the market to exchange their produce for a different kind of produce of others.

Smith assumes that capital simply exists; there is no investment to be made, at least at first. No provision for capital means, by extension, that there is no debt to service an asset that formed the capital, including land. The owner is the employee, and the employer is the owner. Like a medieval age craftsman or like today's self-employed electrician, or plumber, he brings in his tools and machines to do the work. Hence the basis for concluding his idea of the market structure as a capital-less, debt-free, labor-free, land-absent type of system. Everything happens in a vacuum.

The production output of all economic activities in the world during the Age of pre-Industry and the world to which thinkers like Smith belonged was nothing more than the day-to-day produce – on the whole mainly the output of trademark traditional economic activities. As it is, the output of traditional activities being technology-free means the uncertainty factor that unceasingly characterizes industries manufacturing technology-imbedded products that originally were a gift from the Age of Industrial revolution had mostly been a mystic to thinkers like Smith. They belonged to a world that did not have heavy industry. Given that, the economic system – the capitalist system of production and exchange – to Smith's mind is merely a grand barter arrangement of technology-free products and services in which nobody loses, and everybody wins, apparently due to the invisible hand's role in smoothing out the self-interest parties of the market.

That construction of Smith's view of the market laid above is reasonable and to the point, notwithstanding the fact that at other places in the book Smith wrote at length on labor productivity (the pin factory), on land, on savings to use for capital. But in the market structure those are assumed as given, and not to be bothered when the discussion centers on the distribution aspect of the economic system, which as a matter of history of mainstream economics, had become the system as a whole. When the question of distribution comes, the issue of production goes silent, as Smith's writings and theories of those who approved that line of thinking and built on it show.

Based on exactly such a description of the market I laid above, the two mid-twentieth century economists Kenneth Arrow and Gerard Debreu set out to prove mathematically that the invisible hand of the market produces Pareto optimal outcomes. Since then, economists have identified their breakthrough 1954 paper "Existence of an Equilibrium for a Competitive Economy" as the long-awaited and final mathematical proof confirming the efficiency of Smith's invisible hand, or of the market system in general.

It is understandable that political economists writing before the advent of the Industrial Revolution had failed to grasp the idea of products that embed technology, and the concept of uncertainty. The existence of technology products and uncertainty permeating the industrial economy penetrate into the decision-making process of the investing individuals and entrepreneurs. It is only shameful that even since the times after the fruits and miracles of technology had laid bare for all to see, the concept of uncertainty emanating from heavy industry appeared unattractive to the minds of the economist-intellectuals. Why not? Smith's conception of markets with all kinds of certainty has proven to be more compelling. Only John Maynard Keynes in his 1936 magnum opus *The General Theory of Employment, Interest, and Money*, and Joseph Schumpeter in his 1942 book *Capitalism, Socialism and Democracy* had brought up the concept of Uncertainty and shed some light on the profound role it plays in industrial economies.

Besides the gross errors committed by painting a simplistic picture of the modern economic system, the contents of the system – or the integral parts, so to say – have been scrubbed to arrive at the idea of one commodity and one individual as the basis of all economic analysis. As identified in Chapter Four, the three fictitious commodities of the market – land, labor, and money – are just another commodity to this model. The errors identified thus far – all of them resulting simply from a grossly incorrect identification of the structure of the market as it existed and exists. The errors laid bare here extend to the moving parts of the system too, as we'll see.

In the Capitalist economic system, the factors of production necessarily comprise land, labor, capital (other than land such as machinery), money (working capital), raw materials, and process know-how. It is labor that is not only a factor of production but also an income-receiving factor along with the factor of capital. That is an income with purchasing power to demand products whose production was the source of the income. Within the composition of National income, Capital income and Labor income take the name thus.

Thus, the flow of income that begins with the production splits and goes to the labor and the capitalists in the form of labor income and capital income, and this income, then, demands in aggregate the entirety of the same products their machinery and hands helped manufacture.

In fact, a key role that banks play is the facilitation of the first transaction that starts the circular flow of income. If one needs to receive income before one spends, and this condition is true for all market participants, then the system is stuck; this is where banks as part of the economic system create credit money out of thin air that helps start the cycle of income and spending. We'll discuss more about modern banking system later on.

The system with this kind of feedback loop – where income from production is spent on the same products that they (capital owner and labor) had a hand in the making (spread across various manufacturing plants and service centers) – may appear (so far as I laid out) to be identical to the grand barter exchange system, but I seem to imply otherwise.

Where previously the individual craftsmen and the sole-employer producer came to the market to exchange their produce with others, they merely traded the income they earned from selling their produce for that of others. In that system of barter exchange, total income received is also total expenditure incurred by spending on a different kind of produce. One's produce, say, of milk, is exchanged for eggs, meat, pins, etc. The producer of eggs may exchange it for something else, a bag of goods. Now, one may juxtaposed the above case I had laid out with Smith's barter system to conclude that the presence of labor, as an employee to the owner-producer, is just another owner-producer organized differently under the banner of employee. And also that, the labor or owner-producer is receiving no less income for the part in the production process in either case. Henceforth, it may appear that there is no such gross distinction between the two systems. However, that is not the whole story. In fact, the feature that so starkly diverges Smith's world from real world is that one element that is the basis for the construct that we call Capitalist Economic System.

The Capitalist Economic System

The uniqueness of the factor of labor, identified to be one among the three fictitious commodities of the market, is one such important divergence in the functioning, real world, capitalist economic system from Smith's world of barter exchange system. Another divergence corresponds to the process. Whereas in Smith's world, all income is bartered for other produce, in the functioning real world, of the income received in the form of Capital income or Labor income, a portion is "saved." A world in which people save escapes the narrow construction of mainstream economic models to this day.

National Income is composed of consumption and saving, where a portion of income not consumed is savings, and National spending is composed of consumption and investment, where the share of spending that is not going to consumption is going for investment. That breakdown is pure accounting, valid for any individual or household as well. An individual's annual income of, say, USD 50,000 is split into USD 40,000 of consumption and USD 10,000 of saving; it also means that the same individual's annual spending is USD 40,000 on consumption and 10,000 as an investment (sitting as a bank deposit perhaps). The annual income is equal to annual spending. In the case of nations (even individuals who borrow), that may not be the case, as spending could be more or less than income depending on whether the nation is borrowing from or lending to other countries (the difference between the two equations of income and spending plus the net factor income received from abroad equals a nation's current account).

In Smith's world, all income goes to consumption and therefore, all spending as well on consumption. That just is not the case in the world we live in. This notion of the grand barter exchange system of the market advanced by Adam Smith deceived great many. Consider Fig 11.1 illustrating the functioning capitalist economic system, containing the nexus between national wealth and economic activity. In the envisioned world of Adam Smith, the economic system at most resembles the bottom part depicting the cyclical flow of income and spending: income sourced from the production of consumer goods becomes the source of consumer spending enabling consumption. It is essentially a systematic course of income flow without the interruption of savings culminating into a non-stop goods exchange system. However, this make-believe world of Smith is far apart from the complex and dynamic functioning capitalist economic system, which for the most part is captured in the snapshot that is Fig. 11.1.

The income originating from the production of consumer goods on its way to consumer spending a portion of it escapes in three different directions, asset investment, savings, and consumer imports. The remaining portion of this income circulating in the loop unhindered is joined by spending from three different directions, consumer spending by owners and workers belonging to the capital goods industries, exports, income from asset liquidation, culminating into spending on consumer goods whose production the source of a stream of new income.

The income moving in the direction of asset investment is essentially the management of current income in the direction of purchase of assets created prior. That means, for example, in the functioning system the wages or profits earned the preceding month – as part of the income flow of the running year – acts as down payment or full payment for the purchase of an asset. That asset may be a house built in 1980 or a 30-year corporate bond issued originally in 2012. That amount of wages or profits routed to the purchase of an asset may emerge back into the spending loop of the running year as consumer spending (or capital investment) by the asset-seller or someone down the line of sale.

The savings that escaped from the Loop A enter the bank to emerge out as a loan to entrepreneur or homeowner for capital spending that result in capital investment. The capital goods industries receive revenue from three different directions, capital spending by entrepreneur or homeowner, exports, depreciation expenditure by all operating businesses – the first two constituting expenditure on new capital investment, whereas the last one to replace a portion of the accumulated and old capital. The income accrued by the production agents, capitalists and labor, belonging to the capital goods industries, then escapes into three different directions, asset investment, savings, and consumer imports, just as the income originating from consumer goods industries does, with the rest chasing consumer goods.

As is evident from the figure, a portion of revenue accrued by both the consumer goods and capital goods industries is set aside for depreciation expenditure. This amount does not constitute income of anyone. The wear and tear on the factory floor requires replacement. Therefore the depreciation expenditure chases capital goods– the output of the capital goods industries. That means, say, a hydraulic excavator manufacturer– a capital goods industry, is depreciating a portion of the physical assets of the business by the purchase of CNC (Computer Numerical Controlled) lathe machine or boring machine from the machine tool manufacturing business that also belongs to capital goods industry. All operating businesses have assets that depreciate over time.

Figure 11.1 – Functioning Capitalist Economic System

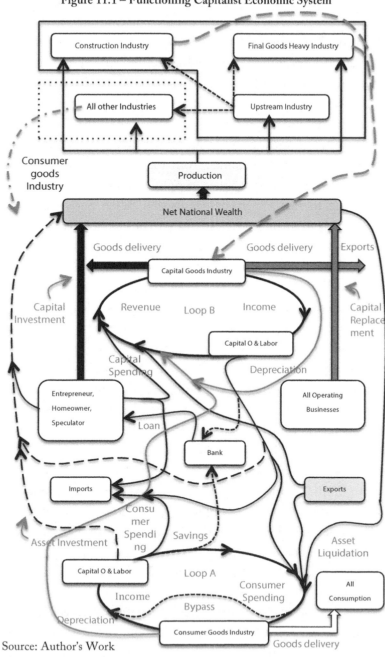

Source: Author's Work

The expenditure on depreciation as shown in the figure results in the delivery of capital goods replacing the old capital. The capital income and labor income that emerge from the revenue diverges into savings and spending, just as the income earned from the production of consumer goods does. The Fig 11.1 adequately captures the real-world functioning Capitalist Economic system.

Another classical economist, the Frenchmen Jean-Baptiste Say (1767 – 1832), claimed, on top of Smith's supposed workings of the market, that supply creates its demand, or something to that effect (this is usually called Say's Law). In Say's world, all income from the supply (production) comes back to demand those goods. True, but only in a fictional world where people don't or can't save. There is some confusion as to what Say actually said or meant, but irrespective of what he implied, there is no denying that supply does not create its demand.

The distinction, as I pointed out and illustrated in Fig 11.1, is that in the real world, people who earn labor income or capital income save a portion of it. That is important because this aspect (saving, and borrowing and lending) is the link between the income statement, and the balance sheet, be it of an individual, business, or a country. Therefore, it is the key to understanding many economic phenomena that mainstream economics had been so inept at addressing.

In Smith's world of barter exchange system, there is only an income statement with a simple consumption option. Balance sheet's absence is the same as identifying this world to be capital-less, debt-free and land-less.

The USD 10,000 sitting in that individual's bank account is recorded as an asset under the right side of the individual's balance sheet, just as a country's new investment financed by new savings becomes an asset, and can be counted as new wealth (or capital) endowed to the country. When an individual or a country borrows to spend on investment, the asset side goes up by that much (at the time of the purchase of the asset) of the borrowed funds that in parallel added on to the liability side (left) of the balance sheet as "long-term debt".

Where national income is the sum of all annual income receipts, and likewise national spending, on the aggregate the national wealth or national capital is the sum of net wealth of all private individuals, the civic institutions (which no individual even indirectly owns, such as charities), and the government.

But the accounting compositions of income, spending, balance sheet may appear similar for the individual and the country, but the way in which composition for a nation is arrived differs starkly from that of the individual. First, let's take up the Balance sheet. There is a simple aspect that needs to be cleared up here, and this is nothing new. Assume for simplicity, that person A and person B, each own USD 100,000 in net worth (assets-liabilities), and that these two comprise the entire nation. Now the country's net worth, in extension, merely is USD 200,000 – a simple balance sheet for the country. But the two individuals themselves can loan money out of their wealth to the other, creating assets and liabilities in unlimited numbers onto their balance sheets, all by keeping the overall net worth of the country the same as before. A can lend USD 50,000 to B, thereby creating an asset of that much value on the balance sheet of A, and an equal value of debt liability on the balance sheet of B. Next B loans A USD 75,000. That creates an asset on B's balance sheet, and a debt liability on A's balance sheet, in the fashion similar to the first transaction. Such a scenario does not change the overall net worth of the country. The physical capital or the wealth of a country remains the same before and after those transactions. The wealth of a nation expands only upon new capital investment.

In practice, some private individuals purchase a ten-year bond newly rolled out by a national retail chain, thereby creating an asset on the bondholder's balance sheet, and a debt liability of the same value on the retailer's. Later, the value of the bond fluctuates based on market mood, thereby changing the asset value on the bondholder's balance sheet, and by extension, the bondholder's net worth as well.

Likewise, the value of an asset on the balance sheet changes in conjunction with the market. The value of an asset such as a house may go up or decline; the value of the stocks may similarly change. Such vagaries do project onto the balance sheet, and the corresponding forces projected onto the income statement, and therefore by extension, on consumption, savings, and investment decisions– all of those factors are part of the two equations, individual income and individual spending.

To sum up, the individuals' income statement and balance sheet are interlinked in such a way that the state of the balance sheet affects the decisions made on consumption, savings, and investment. This construction of the economic system of the world, when observed in practice, is starkly distinct from that envisioned by Adam Smith. The simplistic notion of markets since Smith caused people into believing that the market is fully capable of self-regulating. And in the same abundantly useless technical language of economics, while the market may lapse out of equilibrium at times, as it did in the aftermath of the 1929 Stock Market Crash, the market could restore to the equilibrium in no time– it was heartily believed. In the persistent failure of liberal democratic politics, the economic consequences of the crash inevitably led to political consequences, as we have discussed at length in earlier Chapters.

Failure and Utopia

The classic failure of Classical Liberalism is the utopian fantasy it constructed from the visual portions of the then Western economic system that turned out to be grossly simplistic at best in theory and suicidal at worst when it served as the basis to see and understand reality. The underlying claims being that the Self-regulating market provides greatest economic freedom for self-interested individual agents and works to the effect of most efficient deployment of resources, but also happens to provide the greatest good for all. The flaw with Self-regulating market notion lies not with its commitment to and upholding of greater economic freedom for the individual as compared to any other economic system but that it is a construct and a derivative of a mental conjecture that has no place in practice.

Quite amazingly, the Self-regulating market in practice is the vehicle that gives into economic anarchy in which individual's economic freedom is meaningless. An apt metaphor, but by no means a perfect one, is that of the general order of the individual and individual freedom in society. A propulsion to outright ultimate freedom of the individual to the extent that the state had been disbanded may give into a brutish, miserable life; as any one individual may feel free to prey on another, freedom evaporates and chaos begins. The organization of economic system in the mode of Self-regulating utopia of the market is nothing but a transparent veil of anarchy gripping the society in the claws of misery and ruin.

Only by first regulating money and then labor and land, shall the market cease to function to the ends of a utopian project. That it is when the state begins to regulate the creation and supply of domestic currency, unhinged from the inherently arbitrary moods of functioning systems such as the gold standard or more clearly from the relic of the past, gold itself; and provide for the dignity and safety of labor at the workplace; the availability and treatment of land, that the self-interested individual shall be endowed with the greatest economic freedom. The role of the state coming to protecting life and property in the matters of society is akin to the role in the issues of the economy. The state role extends to safeguarding and regulating the limited supply of the three commodities – one of the three having been endowed with life itself, another related to nature on which life and the construct of family inextricably depends, and the third that greases the relationship between the first and second.

Here is where economic thinkers cratered. The economic and technological upheavals of the times – the industrialization and the accompanied modernization of economic activity in a country – posed this simple task to the economic thinker: to design a theory that conclusively explains the macro and micro workings of economic activity, the relationship between them, and the relationship between national income and national wealth (and in extension, between national income and the debt to service the capital), the role of money, banking, and international trade and exchange, and the consequences these have on such critical aspects of human prosperity as employment, wages, profits, return on capital, savings and spending, growth. But economic thinkers faltered; they produced theories that only had a place in utopian dreamlands. Even as the recent financial crisis had passed by and not a credible theoretical reasoning had been put forth to explain the ultimate causes fully.

Amidst such demonstrable failures in the realm of economic theory over the past two hundred years now, there is no credibility left to mainstream ideas concerning the economic dimension of the society. In 2016 and 2017 the events of upheaval, flirting with and conquering Western countries, lay in the historical forces that remain unexplained anywhere. The most recent and profoundly transformative event was the financial crisis; and as it is, all miseries, dogma, and failure grip the event. It is only by precisely understanding what caused the crisis can we fathom the future of Western civilization more clearly. Therefore, we'll take up next the causes of the financial crisis. I follow that part with a final Chapter summarizing the critical developments of the past two-hundred years and extending the larger forces operating unseen and influencing consequential events – like the financial crisis – to the future and get a glimpse of what lies ahead.

Chapter Twelve

The Ultimate Causes of the 2008 Financial Crisis

The End of Industrialization & Modernization

To recall, National capital is classified into these four types: Housing capital, Public infrastructure capital, non-Industrial business capital and Industrial business capital. Further, business activities carried out under the technical umbrella of non-Industrial business capital belong to traditional economic activities. The accumulation of this class of capital signals gradual modernization of a country, whereas the accumulation of Industrial business capital essentially underscores the process of industrialization that through the supply of machinery and equipment facilitates modernization. The process of modernization simply means investment in and installation of machinery and equipment by non-industrial businesses. The Age of Industrial Revolution across the West began roughly in 1867 and ended in 1913 due to the start of war the following year. Thanks to few rapid discoveries since the turn of the twentieth century, modernization program began to accelerate primarily in the United States, but only later amply in Europe.

By all means, this gradual pace of investment to upend the way traditional economic activities have been carried out since time immemorial ended with the first oil crisis in 1973. This trend is evident in the gradual decline of US savings rate since 1973, as seen in Fig 12.1 showing annual savings rate for the United States from 1940 to 2007. The saturation of investments concerning modernizing economic activities meant few direct new investment opportunities remained within the country.

Figure 12.1 – United States National Savings Rate 1940 – 2007

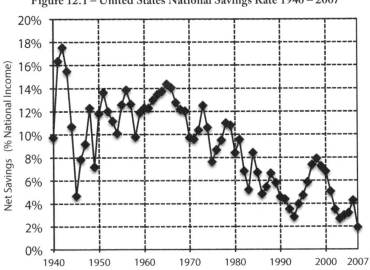

Source: Alvaredo Facundo, Anthony B. Atkinson, Thomas Piketty, Emmanuel Saez, & Gabriel Zucman, *The World Wealth and Income Database* 2016 <http://www.wid.world>

That is, to the minds of businesses and entrepreneurs the investment opportunities that arose from modernization within the boundaries of the country saturated. This trend is just as same in the case of France, the UK or Germany. Unfettered savings is not a permanent feature of any economic system. Investment opportunities saturate as soon as the needs are met. Industrialization and modernization were just like that. It was with the advent of the industrial revolution that modernization became possible. The dual existence of limits to savings rate (savings as a percent of national income) – both in the historical run and in the rate in a given year – is one of the major discoveries in my book *The General Theory of Rapid Economic Development*. Another macroeconomic law that shall be used for the discussion at hand is: it is the aggregate net investment that determines the overall net savings (during any given period that may be a year or a quarter). John Maynard Keynes first proposed this law in his magnum opus in 1936. However, it is unrecognized in the validity or unappeased in the derivation of the law by mainstream theorists, let alone in the extent and range of its utility. For our purposes – that is in the context of Western countries that have industrialized early on and have modernized – the momentum in the savings rate figure slipped from 8% and above to roughly 8% and below after both processes had effectively ended.

The saturation of capital investment within a country in the two classes of business capital, namely non-Industrial business capital and Industrial business capital had profound consequences. The traditional means of accumulation of profits and higher returns by an investment in a business venture allowing for annual profits and return of capital, in the long run, had come to a halt. The only possible class of capital that could provide unceasing investment and returns remained housing capital and public infrastructure capital. However, about the latter class of capital there exist myriad inherent barriers that do not allow for endless investment by private entrepreneurs. It is quite easy to underscore few of them. Foremost, the range of public infrastructure requirement, in the broadest sense, is limited by lifestyle, geography, and population distribution, etc. in a country. Interstate highways are possible; intra-city highway and roadway links, parks, bridges, tunnels, street roads, other public utilities are a common feature. Once the range of options and needs are met, there exist few other requirements that call for new public infrastructure spending.

What's more, public infrastructure investment is carried out mostly under the provision and direction of local and state governments. Investment spending in public infrastructure to the mind of a private entrepreneur is distinctly cumbersome as compared to investment in other businesses, if not for it being

Figure 12.2 – Net Investment Rates of Germany, France and US 1970 – 2015

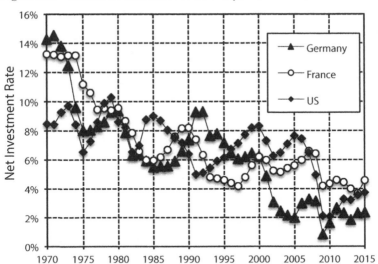

Source: Author's own calculations based on the National Accounts data of the United States, France, and Germany. Note: Data of Germany Prior-1990 is of West Germany

regulated and limited by local and state governments. With non-Industrial business capital and Industrial business capital reaching saturation, and Public infrastructure capital limited and regulated by the government, housing capital remained as the only remaining class of capital that had room for new investment.

Figure 12.2 shows net investment rates for the three major economies, the US, Germany, and France from 1970 to 2015. In the postwar era, the two mainland European countries that lagged the US in modernization accelerated the process. Additionally, as a result of the world wars and foreign occupation, the reconstruction of destroyed capital meant the two nations posted high net investment rates (new [net] investment as a share of the annual GDP). Therefore their rates hovered above 12% and higher, as compared to that of the US entering into the 1970s.

But the signs the processes of industrialization and modernization coming to an end is evident from Fig 12.2 as investment rates declined well into the 10% rate and below. In fact after 1974, never again any of the three countries had posted an investment rate higher than 12%, as is clear. As East Germany and West Germany were united, the need for new investment in the East Germany territory meant Germany witnessed a significant upswing in investment rate around the 1990s. In the fifteen years since the millennium, the rate never eclipsed past 8% figure for any of the three.

Thus regarding new business investment opportunities, there had left housing capital as the only type of capital for investors to pour money into. However, despite seeing saturation in regards to business capital, there had also existed an alternative avenue for possibilities of handsome returns on investment: speculation on assets (the stock of accumulated capital) that already exists. Both kinds of business capital and housing capital qualify– shares or stocks of businesses, houses and condominiums. Concerning business capital, shares or stocks such as those of General Electric, Apple, Caterpillar (industrial) or JP Morgan, Comcast, Wal-Mart (non-industrial) already existed to engage in speculation by an individual or an institutional investor. However, regarding speculation on housing capital, it fell on the financial industry to devise requisite framework and mechanism to engage in the same.

The Age of Electronics Industry & Speculation

Before we go further concerning speculation, we need to discuss the one industry that had left open an avenue for direct new investment in business capital even after the Age of Industrial revolution had long passed, and the Age of Modernization had ended. That new industry was the electronics industry, a derivative from the Age of Late Electronics Revolution that began in the postwar years. The development of particle physics – due to the two world wars – in effect lagged the inventions central to the electronics industry. The transistor, the integrated circuit chip, the graphical user interface, and the mouse remain at the heart of computer revolution that ushered in new business opportunities for entrepreneurs.

Henceforth, since the Age of Modernization ended these were the avenues for businesses, entrepreneurs and investors to make investment: new investment in electronics industry, new investment in housing, speculation on all possible capital – (including speculation on the items on the balance sheet of all such businesses that own the capital, such as bonds) including non-Industrial business capital and Industrial business capital, housing capital, including new capital of electronics industry and even new housing capital (that is those houses built during the recent times, and not long time ago). It sums up to this: investment making avenues left open are new investment in electronics and housing, and speculation on all classes of existing and accumulated assets and capital except public infrastructure capital.

The 1980s and the 1990s was the era that saw investment pouring into all kinds of electronics businesses. After the instability of the 1970s, caused in no small extent by the two oil price hikes in 1973 and 1979, the low inflation era that began since 1980s laid the groundwork for continued speculation on capital – including stocks, bonds, housing capital. It is not a coincidence that Wall Street became powerful during this time. Speculative and business investment activities, including investment in electronics, reigned the era as NASDAQ – the stock exchange geared for electronics corporations – peaked, and also the NYSE hit all-time highs.

The long boom from the early 1980s to the first months of 2000 saw stock prices of all classes of the capital surge, as the speculative binge was financed or serviced by ever-rising financial debt.

When stock prices rose up year-after-year, increasingly detached from the underlying profit-making potential of the businesses in question, the slide to the bottom – or what is called the correction – was only natural and inevitable. Thus the speculative binge on stocks of the 1990s fueled due in part by the enthusiasm that came from the availability of genuine new investment opportunities in electronics, hit the sealing in March 2000. During the 1990s, the financial industry devised mechanisms to speculate on housing capital, just as speculation on business capital is done using business shares and stocks. Mortgage Backed Securities (MBS)– a rated asset, backed by chunks of underlying diversified home mortgages newly underwritten by banks, came to be the medium that allowed for safe investment in the housing market.

The intensity of speculation on assets– or the buying and selling of assets using leveraged debt can be evidenced from Fig 12.3. The spikes in the capital gains income (as a percent of aggregate annual national income) of the top one-percent income earners in the year preceding the 1987 stock market crash, the year of the 2000 NASDAQ crash, and the 2008 financial crises, manifestly show the speculative bonanza. The massive spike before the postwar World, as may be noticed, occurred in the year preceding the 1929 Stock Market Crash. The horizontal line drawn as a reference at the value of 1.36% is the average annual capital gains income of the top one-percent between 1933 and 1978.

Figure 12.3 – US Top One percent Capital Gains Income 1920 – 2015

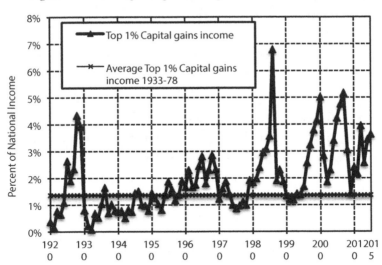

Source: Alvaredo Facundo, Anthony B. Atkinson, Thomas Piketty, Emmanuel Saez, & Gabriel Zucman, *The World Wealth and Income Database* 2016 <http://www.wid.world>

As the NYSE and NASDAQ rally and the spending binge on the new electronics businesses cratered after March 2000, the demand for new MBS for speculation exploded. The underlying value of each MBS rests on a set of chunks of mortgages meant demand for new MBS drove demand for new housing projects. As it is, when electronics industry offered the last avenue for new investment within the business capital spectrum, the housing capital itself stood alone when opportunities in electronics saturated. Therefore, net savings – that amount that finances new investment in a given year – increasingly routed into the housing market in the US since 2000. The trade deficits financed the shortfall in the aggregate investment. So not only the housing market remained an avenue for pouring new savings, but also the new financial assets (MBS) created out of this binge, having similarities with the business stocks, met the demand for

Figure 12.4 – US Personal Assets Value 1913 – 2013

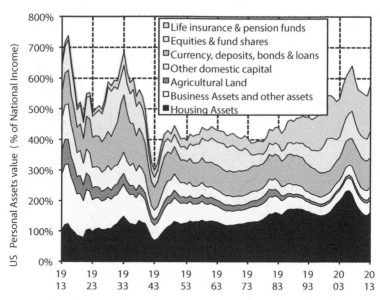

Source: Alvaredo Facundo, Anthony B. Atkinson, Thomas Piketty, Emmanuel Saez, & Gabriel Zucman, *The World Wealth and Income Database* 2016 <http://www.wid.world>

debt-financed speculation on capital. This sweet nexus in supply and demand rapidly fueled prices of houses to increasingly higher levels, even of the houses constructed before the turn of the new millennium.

The debt-backed housing investment by homeowners (who also engaged in speculation, flipping houses) and the debt-backed MBS speculative investments that indirectly underwrote the new houses in question foreshadowed the massive speculative binge on business stocks in the two decades since the turn of the 1980s. The exploding value in housing prices is evident from Fig 12.4 showing the US personal assets value for each year from 1913 to 2013. The aggregate value of all housing stock in the US rose substantially from the mid-1990s to all the way leading up to the crisis in 2007.

Figure 12.5 – US Personal Debt Value 1913 – 2013

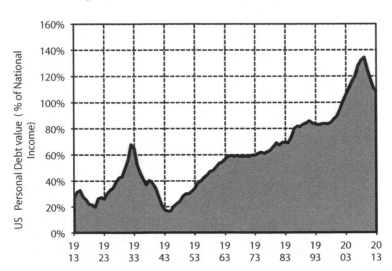

Source: Alvaredo Facundo, Anthony B. Atkinson, Thomas Piketty, Emmanuel Saez, & Gabriel Zucman, *The World Wealth and Income Database* 2016 <http://www.wid.world>

As house prices, driven by both phenomena, rose month-after-month, year-after-year wholly detached from reality – the term "reality" to be understood as similar to the meaning construed from the context of businesses whose future profits underscore the reality – the cratering effect proved that much disastrous since new investment and speculation were debt-financed. See Fig 12.5 showing US personal debt value for each year from 1913 to 2013. As it is clear, the aggregate personal debt – the sum of all outstanding debt held personally by all of the households in the US in the given year – rose monumentally, all the way from about 85% of national income in the mid-1990s to 135% in 2007. That precipitous rise in personal debt funded none other than the housing stock, apart from the business stocks, causing prices to soar. Simply, the money borrowed went to financing the purchase of a home – built many years ago, or built the running year.

The Nexus Between the Balance Sheet and the Income Statement

In general the difference (net worth) between the value of the aggregate assets and that of aggregate liabilities on the balance sheets of millions of households, non-financial businesses, financial businesses, changes with time. And this is primarily due to the change in the asset values, whether in the direction of appreciation or depreciation from the instance of purchase. The negative net worth that arises accidentally or incidentally among the few random entities, at random instances, shall not pose adverse effects on to the economic system, as is the case that underlies the normality. It is when the net worth goes negative for the greater many that do, as we'll see how and why.

When millions of entities, or a higher proportion of the entities of a country, see the value of their assets go up over a period, it necessarily is due to the changing landscape of the particular asset – housing, or stocks, or bonds. In parallel to such an appreciation, the values of all of the assets belonging to such a category also appreciate steadily, and hence the phenomena called "the bubble." The Housing asset turned out to be the vehicle, for reasons we have just explored.

The prices of those assets appreciate only so much as it will always be the case since the bubble is pumped up by debt. As the prices inevitably hit the peak value, the resulting paranoia causes speculators to dump a portion of assets of that same class en-mass only to see the prices depreciate even more. That phenomenon befalls any class of asset, whether it is housing stock or business stock. Many entities, as a result, find

Figure 12.6 – US Corporate Assets 1946 – 2013

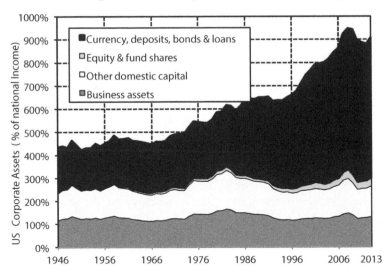

Source: Alvaredo Facundo, Anthony B. Atkinson, Thomas Piketty, Emmanuel Saez, & Gabriel Zucman, *The World Wealth and Income Database* 2016 <http://www.wid.world>

themselves underwater, as the value of liabilities outweighs that of assets on their balance sheets.

Exactly in such fashion, in the lead up to the crisis, the actors such as investment banks, homeowners who took massive loans to purchases unaffordable housing, foreign investors, the insurance companies that guaranteed the risk, all had gone under. Their balance sheets went underwater – that is, their assets valued less than their liabilities – causing panic selling that further heightened the new negative gap between the two sides of the balance sheet for many. In fact, the difference in the values in each year between the Fig 12.4 and Fig 12.5 is the aggregate net personal wealth of all residents in the United States (adding the net worth of non-personal private institutes to this figures gives the aggregate net private wealth of US) for that year. At the peak of rising debt and rising asset values, that is in 2007, the

Figure 12.7 – US Corporate Liabilities 1946 – 2013

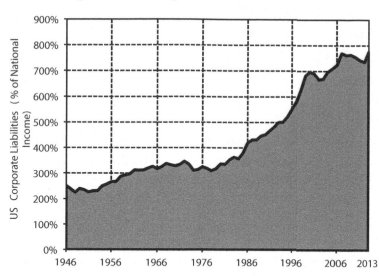

Source: Alvaredo Facundo, Anthony B. Atkinson, Thomas Piketty, Emmanuel Saez, & Gabriel Zucman, *The World Wealth and Income Database* 2016 <http://www.wid.world>

aggregate net personal wealth amounts to about 500% of US national income in 2007, after deducting 135% outstanding personal debt value from about 635% personal assets value for that year. The balance sheets in the proceeding months after the peak sometime in 2007 effectively went underwater for many households – whoever owned assets whose value sunk below the outstanding debt they owed – leaving many other households just fine.

This transpiring of cause and effects in the case of private individuals is no different from the case of US corporations – or specifically the financial institutions including the industrial heavyweights that engaged in financial activities such as GE under its subsidiary GE Capital. See Fig 12.6 and Fig 12.7 showing US corporate assets value and corporate liabilities value respectively for each year from 1946 to 2013 – these figures belong to the balance sheets of all business corporations in the US, whose financial value (the worth of the company) is reflected in the corporation's stock price. The increasingly rising debt taken in by US corporations – from about 500% of national income in the mid-1990s to about 780% in 2007 – reflect on the asset values they had on their books that also rose just about from mid-1990s all the way up to the crisis. This thunderstorm style effect, a purely market phenomena, had caused the balance sheets to go underwater – in the case of both the households and the financial institutions.

This downward effect (negative) on the balance sheet projects onto the income statement of each one of those entities. To correct the wrongs on the balance sheet, that is to offset the difference arising from the sinking asset values underwritten by liabilities, these entities begin the process of paying off the debt that underwrote their asset purchase previously. That drive among the millions of entities to saving in a greater proportion of their income compared to the past means the income earned from the consumer goods production sees falling demand, leading to a further drop in the production volume (see Fig. 11.1 showing the multi-direction split of income flow). And therefore that ensures a further effort among the entities to increase their saving proportion of income, worsening the entire situation.

The Crisis and the Great Recession

In the lead up to the crisis, as the prices of assets hit the ceiling, the falling prices caused the balance sheets of several number of private entities to go underwater. That development in extension had affected the income statements of those entities causing them to reduce their spending and save more to pay off the debt payments and get out of the underwater position they found themselves in; as is only normal, binge saving means lost demand for goods and services bringing in recession very soon.

There is another ripple effect. Having seen falling demand for consumer goods and services, the new investment forthcoming during this period stops as business investors and entrepreneurs delay (why would businesses invest when the existing capital, factories, service centers, is running at less than the regular capacity?). That exacerbates the savings volume being undertaken by the underwater entities, as new investment determines the net savings. Simply how much new investment is undertaken is in effect the value of the savings accumulated. No investment shall mean zero savings forthcoming. Unless of course the production volume about to go down is rescued by a concurrent rise in the export demand, just enough to offset the domestic pressure. For small countries that usually translates into perfect escape route, as large economies feasibly consume exports from small economies. Whereas for large economies, the international arm of the macro-economy is unhelpful. Individual savings still exists even if net savings fall to zero, or close to zero, because that purchasing power translates into consumer spending by another individual who had got his hands on it through his bank via say, credit card. Individual savings gets offset with individual borrowing for consumer spending, and in times like these, borrowing of those funds saved by someone come to be the only recourse to people who saw their income go down little or a lot but their spending did not.

Now in that situation where falling production is being driven by an increased thirst for saving, and therefore further fall in income, the employers at the businesses accordingly let off the employees to smooth out the labor count in accord with the current production volume. As it is clear, this process readily manages to throw off a proportion of the workforce out of the workplace, who as the condition attests shall find hard or impossible to find a new employer. The fall in annual or quarterly national income causes a fall in production that itself caused by an increased thirst for saving among the millions of entities to offset the negative balance on the balance sheets. That shortfall in falling production levels ushers in the recession. And with the rapid collapse of employment, even into a depression.

Of course the economists would lead us believe that one's extra saving to repay the debt is just an income of another who receives the same payment, and hence there is no such thing as turmoil arising from this scenario. However, that line of thinking fumbles in the assumption that the innocuousness of one such prototypical instance translates into many such cases. But it is the attempts at the extra saving in comparison to the previous year's figure, by a sizable portion of the society, in other words, or millions of entities, is the cause of the turmoil. It is because many entities, households and businesses alike, doing the same thing that is the cause of the recession.

Many influential economists and financial journalists firmly believe that the investment binge undertook on new housing since the late 1990s and especially the subprime mortgage lending practice was the decisive factor in causing the financial crisis. However, it was not the aggregate investment in new housing across the United States since the late 1990s that proved to be the problem; it was the corresponding MBS that acted as the primary vehicle upon which the speculative betting was carried. It was not the USD 500,000 home in Austin, Texas that created the underlying systemic crisis but the debt-financed speculation by investment banks, foreign investors on all of those assets containing chunks of the Texas home mortgage claims that did.

To sum up: the Housing stock and to a lesser extent, the business stocks as asset categories served as the perfect platform to engage in speculation by millions of private entities. As a result, that had caused a steady appreciation of the values of houses, existing and new alike, culminating in one of the biggest housing bubbles in history. As the prices hit the ceiling, as they inevitably shall because the debt accumulated only goes so much higher to drive up the prices. The eventual crash of house prices sent the balance sheets underwater causing the collapse of banks and the credit. In the aftermath of this phenomenon, millions of entities started deleveraging to quickly move from negative to positive net worth, resulting from the chain effects into widespread recession and unemployment. If those have been the underlying forces of the recession caused in the aftermath of the collapse of housing and stock prices, the forces operating during the Great Depression were much worse.

The Ultimate Causes of the Great Depression

On top of the above theoretical framework, the addition of an extra layer of misery to this to understand the Great Depression is forbearing. That layer is the International Gold Standard.
As millions of entities try to offset the negative balances on the balance sheet by increasing the proportion of savings out of their income (say, from 40% during the normal-times to 60%), the gold standard had more in store in the unfolding of the financial calamity.

In the above framework concerning the financial crisis, there was an underlying assumption that in the short term the value of currency did not fluctuate significantly. It was given because the monetary system of the postwar world was designed to prevent currency imbalances. Excepting the 1970s, the system worked out well. Therein lies the answer. It was because the pre–Bretton Woods monetary system hinged on gold, the currency instability resulting from it had wrecked the financial system. The deflationary effects pervasive from trading within the system of the International Gold Standard had massively appreciated the value of the nation's currency in nominal terms. That meant a hundred-dollar bill after the deflationary spiral began to fetch more goods than before. With the purchasing power value going up due to money deflation, therefore in the nominal terms, the income earned from all production shall also go down. That is the price of butter and eggs costing previously a dollar each shall now cost only half a dollar each. In Smith's world, this phenomenon is unworthy of attention. How does it matter when person A's produce eggs that cost a dollar each exchanging with person B's produce butter that also cost a dollar, switch to swapping the same eggs and butter that then cost half a dollar each? In the world of barter markets, the denominations shall merely serve as an exchange mechanism.

But in a world where there is capital, and therefore debt, and also therefore the existence of a nexus between the balance sheet and the income statement, the deflationary spiral of the nominal income means knockout blow to the efforts to save a proportion of the increasingly deflating nominal income while having a size of debt on the left side of the balance sheet that is written in absolute unchanging nominal currency terms. That is, compared to the annual income of USD 1000 for an individual last year, the deflating annual income of USD 900 this year is also empowered with the same purchasing power as that of the previous year that is. That deflated income can purchase a thousand eggs with USD 900 when USD 1000 was required in the previous year to do the same. But the individual's plan to increase the savings proportion from last year's 40% to 60% for the current year to meet the debt payments fetches merely an extra USD 140, a loss of USD 60 to the debt reduction scorecard.

The asset bubble created by the debt-backed speculation and the effects of the deflationary forces on the US dollar are manifestly clear in figures 12.4 and 12.5. In Fig. 12.4 showing US Personal Assets values, the value of the aggregate assets as a percent of national income peaked from about 500% in 1923 all the way up to 600% in 1929 just before the stock market crashed and the asset bubble burst. But the curve instead of declining further went up all the way for another few years, as the value of the aggregate assets as a percent of national income eclipsed toward 700% and peaked in 1933. The increase from 600% to 700% is staggering, but this is only because the US dollar during the same period experienced massive deflation, as the recorded dollar change from 12 months in 1932 was 10% (see Fig 4.1). A declining numerator (aggregate asset value) but a much faster declining denominator (national income in the nominal terms) is the reason behind the eclipse from 600% to 700%. It may be noted that as the dollar decline was contained from 1933 – the inflation rate jumped between 1% and 5%, and with slight deflation again in 1937 (a year of recession), the dollar only remained in the upper limits – the US personal asset value kept crumbling down hitting 300% by 1943. This trend is just about the same for the corresponding US Personal Debt – a sharp increase in the aggregate debt value (as a percent of national income) all the way up to 1929, and with the start of massive deflation, a further dramatic increase. Consumers saddled with too much debt faced extra pressure to save their nominally deflating income to pay off the debt payments, and hence the depression.

By a simple measure, new employment is proportionate to new investment undertaken, which itself is due to the perception from a prospective increase in the demand for products produced out of such investment. Hence, in the normal times the inadequacy of, or the shortfall in, the aggregate annual new investment to effectively match the hiring of the unemployed continues, barring state intervention by deficit spending that can provoke more demand and hence increased investment flow.

In the unusual times such as in the aftermath of the bursting of an asset bubble, to offset the negative or crumbling net worth by paying off debt, millions of entities take extra saving measures. As a result, the loss of demand, and in extension the decline of the production, and the income itself means a declining gross output. The miraculous way every year national savings and national investment, arising both as a result of decisions by millions of individuals, takes place in no other way than through the influence those decisions shall have on the income flow and the production decisions on the factory floor.

The functioning capitalist economic system as we have come to understand is far removed away from the simplistic barter world notions of Adam Smith, whose ideas steeped deep into the minds of many professional economists since then.

It comes down now to ask the inevitable question arising from this plethora of figures that have been laid out for private individuals as well as corporate entities in this Chapter concerning recessions and depressions. Where had this much money – in the order of trillions – had come from that effectively paved the way for private individuals and corporate entities to load up mountains of debt on to their balance sheets? The answer – absolutely, and surprisingly to the surprise of mainstream economists – lies in the fact that the modern fractional reserve banking system (in the Age of fiat money) allows commercial banks to create new money out of thin air. Yes, banks can create as much money as by piling up the stock of loans given to its customers. As banks create new loans, they end up with new corresponding assets (the corresponding loans given to the customers) on to their balance sheets effectively adding to the banking business a new stream of income. That is why most of the money in the United States exists not as paper but as bank deposits. Each new deposit made by a bank to a borrowing customer comes out of thin air – the bank writes (credits) the loan amount to the customer's deposit account just like that. It is only after creating this new loan that the bank scrambles to find reserve money by the reserve ratio rules monitored and regulated by the central bank, the Federal Reserve. Thereby the reserve ratio being the only mechanism other than a borrowing customer and the risk of the bank itself going underwater on that particular transaction after seeing the customer go bankrupt that effectively acts as limiting agent to bank's capacity and power to create money out of thin air.

A trustworthy customer is all the bank needs to create a new loan – no need for an equivalent amount of money for it to have in the lockers before signing out on loan. The modern bank is not a clearing-house in which person A's deposit is used to loan money to person B. It is a money creator and different from other business entities precisely because of this characteristic. The modern-day banking system is a throw away from the pre-fiat money era. The gold standard restricted the banks from creating so much easy money without having the adequate gold to back it up, thus the much smaller and subdued debt mountain in the lead up to the Great Depression years than that of the same in the lead up to the Great Recession years. Debt-backed speculation was curtailed after the Roosevelt administration took charge, enacted numerous baking and financial laws, and restricted commercial banks from intertwining business with their investment houses. But with the Great Depression proving much more disastrous on the economy, lives, and society, at least in the aftermath, than the Great Recession ever did, in another way it goes to show the devastating effects of the deflationary spirals of the then monetary system that was the International Gold Standard.

Ironically, it now appears that one kind of banking era – the era of the International Gold Standard – had sunk the West into the Great Depression through its deflationary effects on the money and therefore on all the prices that then spiraled out and worsened the asset bubble burst. And another kind that followed it – the fiat money era – had also sunk the West into another depression-like phenomena, the Global Recession. All too well it seems to come down to money, or more precisely, to understanding the functioning economy fully and properly.

Chapter Thirteen
Liberalism and the Future

A Recap of the Tale of Consequences

The Great War was a conflict that in many ways was the reenactment of the earlier eighteenth century-World War, the Seven Years War (1756 -1763) that spanned five continents and involved all the European powers. Two coalitions of colonial powers, Great Britain and Portugal on one side (along with Prussia and other small German polities like Hanover), and France and Spain on the other side (along with Austria, Sweden, Russia, Saxony, Bavaria) fought for their territorial interests. And it was from that war that Great Britain emerged as the dominant colonial powerhouse, crushing the rival power France. Defeated-power France then succumbed to fiscal ruin and financial turmoil that more so than anything precipitated the French Revolution.

The Great War of the twentieth century itself was a breakout of the clash between German desire for new colonies and Great Britain's desire to consolidate its position as the supreme global colonialist – a position it had held since the treaties were inked ending the Seven Years War. If the fight for colonies was the penultimate cause that precipitated the Great War, then the ultimate cause lay in the economic sphere of these powers. The deflationary forces of the International Gold Standard wrecked all domestic entities, workers and capitalists alike leaving the statesmen with no other option but to pursue a protectionist trade, including such trade with colonies to be newly acquired. The desire for resources coming out of the Age of Industrial Revolution also ran deep.

Thus the Seven Years War and the Great War do not differ much in the penultimate causes of the war – that being the acquisition or consolidation of colonies. And therefore the Great War was not one that came out of nowhere, but it was successive in the long line of battles fought among the European powers for territory. That is why the priority in the use of the term "the Great War" rather than "the First World War" throughout the book; the preference has not been so much an arbitrary choice as it has been about implying that there never really followed a second war from the first. The Great War was just one of the series of successive battles. It was the timing of the war that proved devastating. As the Age of Industrial revolution ushered in industrial-scale manufacturing techniques and technology, the Great War was the first Industrial War. However, it was in the ultimate causes of the Great War that the doctrine of Liberalism tightly fused in the monetary system of the International Gold Standard played the decisive role.

Classical Liberalism – with the peculiarities inherent to it – railroaded the West into the Great War of the twentieth century, causing the Western nations to withdraw into two opposing factions that sought to go to war to resolve the question of dominance once and for all. It should not be overlooked that the West reached its peak, in control and power, of economic and geographic in the sphere, just before the outbreak of the Great War. The West was industrialized and rich; its modernization was going smoothly, and it had control over every inch of the World. The descent of the West since then lay in the forces arising from that which is bound in the ideology of Classical Liberalism, whose failures permuted in practice into the rise of Socialism and all of its applied varieties of Progressivism, Communism, Fascism, National Socialism. The binding theme among all of those reactionary ideologies is their desire and drive toward statism. Marxian Socialism,

National Socialism, and even the postwar Democratic Socialism exemplify every inch of Socialism, varying only by the flavor as denoted by the adjective that was ripe for the conditions of the time.

In the aftermath of 1919 Paris Peace Conference, the chaos and rubble of life and politics fueled the ideology of Socialism of all flavors as they subsequently rose to prominence in the defeated as well as the victorious-but-depleted nations. A state of emergency or chaos, engulfed by the financial calamity or demographic displacement, turned to be just about enough for the ideologue parties to crush the failing and inept liberal politics and seize power. The road to power was paved through democracy. France after the defeat in the Seven Years War had succumbed to financial ruin that precipitated a Revolution, a terror regime, and a military dictatorship. In the same vein, the German financial ruin, characterized by hyperinflation phenomena that destroyed savings and wealth, interspersed with a brief recovery, followed by the Great Depression – whose origins again lay in the return to the International Gold Standard – had precipitated an applied ideology of Socialism called National Socialism into the mainstream early but dormant during the brief recovery period before the depression made their ascent to power and then to dictatorship all too inevitable. Also in the vein of Napoleon – who seized power by overthrowing the French Directory and became the first consul and then the first emperor of France – bent on conquering the entire European landmass apparently to spread and implement the French liberal policies or also known as "the Napoleonic Code," the German circumstances enabled a bloodier, racist ideology and its leader to get elected and to seize and consolidate power and to the application of the ideology on a continental scale.

The breakout of conflict between the two powers – one of them resolved to consolidate the supremacy in the colonial enterprise and another to seize the hegemony by aggressively acquiring the enemy's prior spoils – had resulted in the Great War. Notwithstanding the ultimate causes, it was the fight over territory in the Old World.

The breakout of conflict between the two powers – one of them firmly resolved to expunge the grievous wounds inflicted onto the nation at the peace treaty following the Great War, to conquer and colonize the European Continent itself and another that resisted the megalomaniacal ambitions of the enemy – had resulted in the Second World War that followed the Great War. Notwithstanding the ultimate causes, it was the fight over territory on the European continent itself.

The destruction of the West in the non-Western domain reminds to validate the depths to which Western societies had descended into quagmires that were supposedly waged to consolidate the same – that is, their possessions in the non-Western domain. It is not too hypothetical a claim, therefore, that the Western society had been, and has continued to be in the mode of self-destruction and retreat in the heartland as well all along. Modern Liberalism, the offspring of Progressivism, has culminated amidst the wealth and power in the Age of Modernization into the dominant force for change wrapped in the fight for equality and justice.

If Classical Liberalism railroaded the West into the Great War of the twentieth century, and again (in addition to the wrecked circumstances in the aftermath of the peace treaty and the great depression) into the Second World War, the receding of the West in the non-Western domain was the effect (the outcome of it). But it was Modern Liberalism, as the author and critic James Burnham had shown half a century ago, that functioned to reconcile that receding of the West in the non-Western domain – converting losses into gains of freedom, equality. Moreover, as I have shown in this book, it is Modern

Liberalism that still functions to precipitate and reconcile the fast receding of the West in the Western domain as well.

Classical Liberalism nearly destroyed Western civilization. And even as the Cold War between the US and the Soviet Union – an empire that itself was an unintended byproduct of the practical failures of Liberalism – had exacerbated to a cataclysmic level of nuclear fallout and Armageddon long before and during the Soviet Collapse. Classical Liberalism contended to the destruction of the West in the non-Western domain. Modern Liberalism, while reconciling the West to those losses in the non-Western domain, wasted no time in precipitating the destruction of the homeland this time around.

Classical Liberalism railroaded Western civilization into a conflict between themselves on the supposed missions to prove oneself superior to another. That escalated into two World Wars that later gave into a Cold War. Western civilization had been in a state of retreat since the West began to see the ramifications that Modern Liberalism quietly reconciled the West to it, including even the retreat in the Western heartland.

Simply, Liberalism has had been the greatest hoax ever played on Western civilization.

The Decline of Religion and Modern Liberalism Filling the Void

The previous section was a recap of the world shaped by Liberalism and of the consequences thereof. Throughout the book, we have traced the causation of events of far-reaching significance to the extent that it was feasible to do so. Not only do we now have some knowledge about the causes, both ultimate and penultimate, of the Great War and the Second World War, we have also traced the influence of Liberalism and its contribution in railroading the nineteenth century Western society for failure and collapse. That effectively caused them to dramatically fall back to the point of full-scale conflict and destruction. We have also identified the influence of Modern Liberalism in reconciling the West to its overseas losses, and more importantly, in actively undermining the Western heartland itself.

We have successfully navigated two centuries of history, manifestly influenced by Classical and Modern Liberalism. Let's now turn to a final, important, and larger point regarding the connection that these two centuries – nineteenth and twentieth – have with the preceding and with the succeeding centuries, and to the clue for what lies ahead for the West, and hence the World. Since these two centuries have something to do with the doctrine of Liberalism, it is only logical to ask the question as to the cause of Classical Liberalism, and Modern Liberalism, to understand what is in store.

Classical Liberalism's dialectical features, or more specifically the purposes, have been the Liberal state and the Laissez-faire economy, whereas that of Modern Liberalism has been the Liberal society. Classical Liberalism had gotten the Laissez-faire economy wrong, whose consequences, in parallel to the forces of the Age of Modernization that was due to the Age of Industrial Revolution, enabled the rise of Modern Liberalism.

But Modern Liberalism, whose origins lay in the failure of the laissez-faire front, is on the quest to liberalize the society, but in doing so shall seek the services of, and therefore the sacrifice of the liberal state – the other feature of the predecessor. It is by being able to trace the deep origins of the liberal state itself that the thread connecting the traditional past with modernity and henceforth with postmodernity can be forthcoming.

Religion – more specifically Christianity – has ultimately been the root of the ideals and values cherished, including the sanctity of life and the liberal state that became central to Classical Liberalism and Republicanism. Scientific revolution –

itself an outgrowth of the ideals of individualism of Protestantism – gave way to Industrial revolution, whose transformative effects on domestic economic structure and international trade worsened the inevitable unfolding effects of the laissez-faire economy, the other feature of Classical Liberalism. Darwinism, itself an outgrowth of Scientific revolution, and Socialism, an outgrowth of laissez-faire failure, gave way to intermediary theories whose following form had taken into what we today call Modern Liberalism. Modern Liberalism sacrificed the liberal state to the purpose of liberalizing the society by erasing all traditions including religion, which had been the source of the liberal state in the first place. It indeed is no surprise that there is a common and widespread perception in the West of the daily assault on Judeo-Christian values that have been the characteristic features of Western civilization.

The decline of religion, or of religious influence in the matters of life and culture, in Western societies are uniquely relevant to our times. To get some perspective, the sea of change underway is in regards to the transformation of the role and importance of an institution dating back to roughly 400 AD. The Reformation – itself a movement that strived to form Christianity again in the vein of adhering to the original edicts of the bible – was the only other singular transformative event besides the discovery of the New World that swept the shores of Western civilization until the turn of the nineteenth century. Besides the declining influence of the institution of religion, there is just another non-human force that had been for some time flirting with the West and had already given into momentous events thus far, and about which we'll turn next.

The Decline of Economic Growth and Alternatives Filling the Void

Consider Fig 13.1 showing the GDP per Capita growth for the entire World from 1 AD to 2003. Mainstream economic theories are mostly unhelpful in discerning what this data all means. However, from our discussions in the previous Chapters, we have some knowledge of the economic structure and of the classes of economic activities to dissect the currents of economic forces. It is clear from the figure the sudden upward thrust to per Capita growth rates began around 1820. The pre-Industrial revolution inventions – mostly within the spheres of energy (water turbine), transportation (steam-powered rail), and communication – boosted growth to an unprecedented rate of half a percent on average for about next fifty years, much of it within the Western domain.

The Age of Industrial revolution launched heavy industry that initiated the process of modernizing all traditional economic activities. The per Capita growth rates for the next forty years averaged about 1.3%, again the growth mainly confining within the Western domain.

In the following phase, the destructive wars and tumultuous events such as the Great Depression intervened next bringing down the growth rates below 1%. In the postwar world, the Global South and Global East came to reckon with heavy industry, joining the Western countries' ongoing modernization process that came to a screeching halt in 1973. The high per Capita growth rates in the Global East – notably Japan, South Korea, and Taiwan – in conjunction with the reconstruction programs across Western Europe propelled the per Capita of the World to about 3%. The last phase – the phase to which we still belong – saw a massive drop in the rate from the previous one.

Figure 13.1 – World GDP per Capita Growth 1 AD – 2003

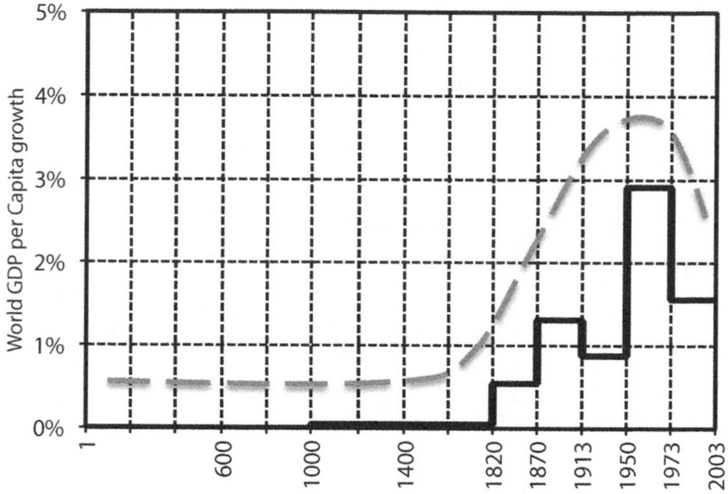

Source: Angus Maddison, *Contours of World Economy 1 – 2003 AD: Essays in macro-economic history* (Oxford: Oxford University Press, 2007)

That was despite the regions of Global South such as the high-growth economies of India, Malaysia and China joining the still high-going East Asian tiger economies South Korea and Taiwan.

That means if it weren't for these high growth economies that have embarked on rapid industrialization drive, growth rates for this phase would have been much lower. See Fig 13.2 that shows GDP per Capita growth for four major early-industrialized countries Germany, France, UK, and the US. The bell curve structure of the average growth rates over this period of close to two hundred years manifests as the phase of the destructive wars between 1913 and 1950 and another phase that saw the last cusp of postwar modernization and capital reconstruction (destroyed in the prior period) between 1950 and 1973 are adjusted and smoothened.

Figure 13.2 – GDP per Capita Growth of Major Early Industrialized
Countries 1820 – 2003

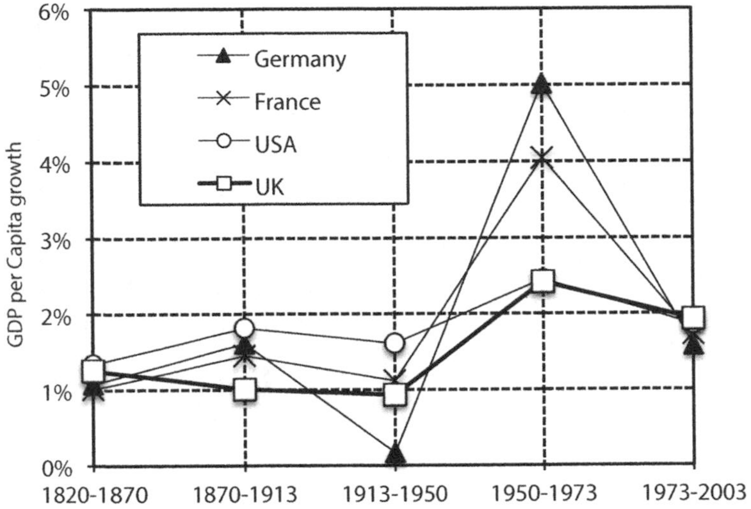

Source: Angus Maddison, *Contours of World Economy 1 – 2003 AD: Essays in macro-economic history* (Oxford: Oxford University Press, 2007)

In the last one-hundred-and-fifty years as the West accumulated capital – the capital of both non-Industrial and Industrial type – the room for new capital investment effectively ended after hitting saturation. Any existing operating business – say, General Electric's power business called GE power – investing in new machinery, say a machine tool called grinding machine – for its plants is effectively using depreciation expenses to install the new and the technologically improved machinery to replace the worn-and-torn. This portion of investment accounts into national spending as part of gross investment and not as part of new domestic investment. It is because of the exhaustion of new business investments that Western firms had sought since mid-1970s to expand their markets further abroad, and therefore having had to force many third world countries to open up to foreign trade – a move carried out under the name of free trade and in practice benefited extraordinarily from the introduction of the "Container box" that revolutionized how goods were transported internationally – and much later since mid-1990s to move capital and manufacturing internationally – a move carried out under the name of free capital flow and in practice benefited extraordinarily from internet allowing international finance and exchange, from advanced and efficient diesel engines powering container ships.

Both moves deluded many into believing that the rise of free trade and free capital flow was a sign of reemergence of market fundamentalism everywhere. This belief only strengthened as the US government itself engaged in financial deregulation in the late 1990s. But this move is again to make room for speculation, as is evidenced by the fact that the deregulating spree focused on particular activities. The Financial Services Modernization Act passed in 1999 repealed a portion of Glass-Steagall Act of 1933 that separated different financial services and prohibited any one single financial institution from acting in any combination of an investment bank, a commercial bank, and an insurance company.

Make no mistake: the future growth rates of Western economies are going to be steeply lower than the average rate seen during typical phases in the past one-hundred-and-fifty years only because the channel for new investments saturated. That phenomenon can be gleaned differently. Unlike what mainstream economic theories lead us to believe, human needs and wants are quite limited and therefore the variety of economic activities to meet and serve those as well. Look no further than Fig 2.1 showing the whole range of economic activities that have been observed in practice classified in a specific manner. The different sections of economic activities falling within an upper class are all limited in number. There are only three broad varieties of activities in primary industry: farming, forestry, and fishing. The secondary industry encompasses activities concerning materials. Mining, construction, and utilities (electricity, gas, water) are specific and recognized from the assigned term. The other section, manufacturing, concerns two kinds of products: one that perishes and does not consume energy (consumer goods), and another that does not perish quickly but consumes energy (machinery & equipment). The second can be put to work to produce output that is related to the rest of the economic activities including itself, such as unearthing minerals and raw materials using mining machinery, erecting buildings using construction machinery, farming using farming machinery, diesel engine powered trucks for transportation services, machine tools like CNC lathe to manufacture mining machinery.

All new gadgets and machinery is an upgrade to the old like. All new varieties of food, drink are a different version of the products that human societies have been accustomed to since time immemorial – the needs and wants have barely changed – hence the term traditional that correctly denotes the activities that offer those. Take services too: healthcare, education, transportation, finance, etc. all go back, and once a level of investment has been allowed into them, in a given country, there no longer arises a requirement to further pour savings into them. All growth in GDP per Capita, if any, results from technological innovation of a given industrial product – say battery, engines, telephone, etc. But even here, the greatest advance in technology already happened with the invention of the plethora of technologies during the industrial revolution itself. Any improvement on an industrial technology since the invention contributes much less to the final form than the invention in the original form ever did. Look no further than the telephone – the invention revolutionized communication as it was introduced in the workable form. The only two improvements seen since then were when wireless technology was married with the telephone creating the mobile "phone," and later computer technology with mobile phone creating the smart "phone."

The Military Might of the United States

It is a comforting idea for many intellectuals that were it not for the aggressive maneuvers of a supreme power, or the mere existence of one such power, world peace would prevail. History challenges and contradicts that claim. As a case study, consider the example of how the changing power structure within the leading powers in Europe at the turn of the twentieth century, one reigning supreme (UK), another consolidating (France), and another emerging (Germany), ignited the idea of a prospective showdown, conflict, and war. The absence of a supreme outside deterrence – a key role the balance of power system played until the collapse – had railroaded them, notwithstanding the ultimate causes, into a grand, bloody war.

The United Kingdom itself acted as the supreme outside deterrence for about a century (the entire nineteenth century), until Germany speeded up preparations to catch up with Great Britain, to match the strength and capacity of the Royal Navy, to challenge its role as the supreme power on the oceans. After the Second World War, the nuclear deterrence voided any direct conflict from emerging between the United States and the Soviet Union. The importance of deterrence cannot be overstressed.

Again, it was the reinforcement of deterrence through the expansion of nuclear weapons by the United States since the early 1980s that indeed precipitated the demise of the Soviet Union. The Soviet Union had collapsed in the desperate attempts to catch up with the US standards amidst the state of an impending bankruptcy. An inevitable financial collapse in the 1970s of the USSR had been avoided, or rather delayed, because of the double lifeline presented to it. The lifelines were the discovery of new oil and gas deposits in the prior decade and the suddenly surging price of oil in 1973. But the collapse of the finances became inevitable once the oil price fell abruptly in the early 1980s. As the depression hit Latin America, the falling demand for oil in one-quarter of the World caused the price to drop. That was a move inflicted and partly instigated by the US Federal Reserve that raised the interest rates exorbitantly to combat the problem of domestic price inflation when at the time many Latin American countries loaded up foreign dollar debt and ready to crumble as soon as real debt payment in dollars went up, as it promptly did.

It is a telling myth that a World, absent of a supreme power that is aggressively wielding force, brings and sustains peace. Only if everyone were disarmed would there be no conflict – a neat dogma disproved by the Dark Ages that followed the decline of the mighty Roman Empire. And it is the Roman Empire's retreat and decline that more than anything Western civilization of the modern times shares parallels. The social decay, people flowing into the heartland, corrupt elites and incompetent rulers, economic imbalances– causing to the ever-declining spirit to fight against the encroaching enemy, spirit to protect the deeply held values and overall, and, most importantly, will to survive.

With the retreat from the within underway, the United States as the supreme military power and the guarantor of peace in the free world had increasingly seen constraints to its might. And that constraint mostly comes down to do with non-material rather than material component.

At this point it would be appropriate to address the role the disproportionate wealth accumulated by the West – as per Credit Suisse Global Wealth Databook (2015), almost 66% of Global Wealth at the end of 2015 is owned by the Western countries that inhabit only roughly 10% of world population. The accumulation of wealth inevitably reaches a threshold – not in the aggregate value but in the variety of capital and in the range of replicating a particular variety. If the range of economic activities is limited as illustrated by Fig. 2.1, then the wealth that underpins the entire economic activity is also limited to that effect and extent. Before the advent of the Industrial Revolution, wealth stock was limited to a large extent to agricultural land and housing. With the advent of the processes of industrialization and modernization, two more stocks of capital attuned to the purposes came to the fore. But the limit has been reached. Thus in what direction the winds of economy blow the human condition is influenced by the phenomena of the West hitting the limits to the stock of wealth accumulation. The course of the West in the past forty years has already been decisively influenced by such a factor, as explored in the previous Chapters.

That brings us to the question of material wealth and power, and resources to defend. Even as the West continues to exist disproportionately wealthy, the decline of the West is an epiphenomenon. That is, the decline is accompanied and caused by non-materials factors that themselves have origins in the Age of Prosperity and Wealth. These non-material factors can be traced to the personal outlook held by the men in the West; his outlook of the West and its history, his priority of values, his will to defend them; and lastly his will to survive. Thus going forward the two major phenomena, non-material in nature, influencing the operating forces is the decline of religion and the softening economic growth rates.

The combined forces of the decline of religion and the softening economic growth rates further down the line across the West lay to a climax that may indeed appear to be very rare. For perspective, the decline of Christianity across the West is a significant phenomenon happening after about sixteen hundred years. In 313 AD by the Edict of Milan, the Roman Emperor

Constantine I gave Christianity a legal status paving the way for its dominance in the Empire and its declaration in 380 AD as the state religion by Emperor Theodosius I. Except for the shakeups of the Reformation, the transformation underway in out times has no precursor or precedent.

Further, the greatest transformative phenomena that hit traditional economic activity – the last of such scope was the agricultural revolution itself couple of thousands of years ago that essentially gave into many classes of traditional activities including farming and finance (debt) – was the Industrial Revolution. The Industrial Revolution had initiated the modernization, but it had come to wind down, with the society already reeling from the consequences of it.

The winding down of Christianity and the softened economic growth rates are the two dual forces of transformation having been underway for few decades now had paved way for the entertainment of Modern Liberalism in the popular mind and provided the impetus to the many missions of erosion the doctrine has tasked itself with including that of seeing the receding of the nation-state. The military might of the United States as that of any other is tied not only to the material resource capabilities but also to the simplest of all, the will to survive and defend. It is against the latter part– the non-material component, Modern Liberalism has been fighting, and it is the status of that element more than that of the material component that shall at the earliest be the critical factor determining the mightiness of the US military upon which peace and freedom so much rest. That prospective development must be understood keeping in mind the historical state of human condition on earth in which the beacon of individual freedom has been a monumental deviation rather than a permanent normal. That must never be forgotten.

Conclusion

On November 8 2016, Americans, with the baby boomer generation turning out overwhelmingly, voted to give the Republican Party the control of the Presidency, ensure they keep their majority in the House and the Senate, and provide an opportunity to tilt the US Supreme Court to the Right. Issues on immigration and trade played a decisive role to hand the Presidency to a businessman and deal-maker who wanted to take control of the porous Southern border and stop the flow of illegals, scrap or renegotiate multi-lateral trade deals, oversee fair trading practices, curtail plant relocations to foreign countries, bring accountability to bureaucrat abuses and drain systemic government corruption.

Since 1992, whenever an American president who had successfully campaigned to win whether as a center, or center Right, or center Left candidate, such as Bill Clinton, or George W. Bush, or Barack Obama, lost his respective Party's majority in the House in the mid-term elections, it was primarily because after his election or reelection he had moved to the Left in the governance and in proposed or enacted legislation. Losing the House majority in the mid-term elections to the opposition after a President takes or retakes office is not preconditioned; it was the voter punishing the President for moving to the Left of the spectrum on issues of trade, immigration, and healthcare, finance. Americans kept rejecting liberal policies year-after-year, election-after-election, but the Democrat Party unable to gain and hold power needed new voters. And thus they have moved to import.

Americans utilized the 2016 General Election to salvage the remnants of the country. Restructuring the immigration programs to benefit the citizens, abdicating from international trade and diplomatic deals designed for special interests, cutting back the regulatory state designed to benefit big corporations, cutting federal income and corporate taxes to alleviate the burden on individuals and families reeling from the effects of the financial crisis, overhauling the federal healthcare insurance law in the direction of subjecting the industry to market forces more, reconsidering the regulations on banks to allow smooth business lending, cutting on the federal bureaucracy and corruption, etc. all represent a move in the direction to relieve the stresses that had built up from the effects of modern liberalism unfolding in the twentieth century and into the twenty-first century.

The retreat of the West may slow down, but the process would not stop, or reverse. There had been no civilization in history once on the path of retreat had turned around to save itself from going down the flames. That law may not be determinative. In this case, Western civilization is tired. It has had a successful run, but the climax has been unfolding for quite some time. The symptoms are there for all to see. Liberals' visceral hatred of the West and of those who made it great in the past or trying to make it great again, and of any efforts to salvage the West exudes as a permanent human feature, unlikely to disappear. Western retreat is being conditioned by outside elements and forces, but it is the lack of wherewithal of the people to stop, reverse, and reemerge that ultimately is detrimental to the kind of outcome we'll see. It is the latter causing the former in practice. The process of the fall of Western civilization is being driven by the immaterial force of Western peoples' unwillingness to defend their own. That is one of self-inflicted and unlikely to cease once it had got going.

Data Sources

Religion, Gallup News, retrieved 19 October 2017, <http://news.gallup.com/poll/1690/religion.aspx>

Mississippi retains Standing as Most Religious State, Gallup News, February 2017, retrieved 19 October 2017, <http://news.gallup.com/poll/203747/mississippi-retains-standing-religious-state.aspx?g_source=position2&g_medium=related&g_campaign=tiles>

Five Key Findings on Religion in the US, Gallup News, December 2016, retrieved 19 October 2017, <http://news.gallup.com/poll/200186/five-key-findings-religion.aspx?g_source=religion&g_medium=search&g_campaign=tiles>

In US Belief in Creationist View of Humans at New Low, Gallup News, May 2017, retrieved 19 October 2017, <http://news.gallup.com/poll/210956/belief-creationist-view-humans-new-low.aspx?g_source=position5&g_medium=related&g_campaign=tiles>

Among Wealthy Nations US Stands Alone in its Embrace of Religion, Pew Research Center, December 2002, retrieved 19 October 2017, <http://www.pewglobal.org/2002/12/19/among-wealthy-nations/>

Americans are in the middle of the Pack Globally when it Comes to Importance of Religion, Pew Research Center, December 2015, retrieved 19 October 2017, <http://www.pewresearch.org/fact-tank/2015/12/23/americans-are-in-the-middle-of-the-pack-globally-when-it-comes-to-importance-of-religion/>

A Growing Share of Americans say it's not Necessary to Believe in God to be Moral, Pew Research Center, October 2017, retrieved 19 October 2017, <http://www.pewresearch.org/fact-tank/2017/10/16/a-growing-share-of-americans-say-its-not-necessary-to-believe-in-god-to-be-moral/>

Bibliography

Data sources have been provided for all graphical representations herein. The combination of analytical nature of the book and first principles theorizing of economic ideas in it had allowed me to supplement the discussion with only a bibliography. The catalog has been curated to include those books that are contemporary and can help you further learn in detail the various ideas and historical developments central to the premise of the book. I refrained from adding any classical works because to include a few would exclude many others that may just as well be fascinating and thought-provoking. Further, it may be best to consult the bibliography in the many books cataloged therein.

Angus Maddison, *Contours of World Economy 1 – 2003 AD: Essays in macro-economic history* (Oxford: Oxford University Press, 2007)

Angus Maddison, *The World Economy: A Millennial Perspective* (Development Centre Studies, 2001)

Ann Coulter, *Adios America: The Left's Plan to Turn Our Country into a Third World Hellhole* (Washington DC: Regnery Publishing, 2015)

Ann Coulter, *Demonic: How the Liberal Mob is Endangering America* (New York: Crown Forum, 2011)

Anne Applebaum, *Iron Curtain: The Crushing of Eastern Europe 1944 – 1956* (New York: Double Day, 2012)

Ben Shapiro, *People vs. Barack Obama: The Criminal Case Against The Obama Administration* (New York: Threshold Editions Subsidiary, 2014)

Ben Shapiro, *Primetime Propaganda: The True Hollywood Story of How the Left Took Over Your TV* (New York: Harper Collins, 2011)

Benn Steil, *The Battle of Bretton Woods: John Maynard Keynes, Harry Dexter White, and the Making of a New World Order* (Princeton, New Jersey: Princeton University Press, 2013)

Brion McClanahan, *9 Presidents Who Screwed Up America: And Four Who Tried to Save Her* (Washington DC: Regnery Publishing, 2016)

Brion McClanahan, *The Founding Fathers Guide to the Constitution* (Washington DC: Regnery Publishing, 2012)

Charles Murray, *Coming Apart: The State of White America 1960 – 2010* (New York: Crown Forum, 2012)

Christopher Clark, *Iron Kingdom: The Rise and Downfall of Prussia 1600 – 1947* (New York: Penguin Books Ltd, 2007)

Christopher Clark, *The Sleepwalkers: How Europe Went to War in 1914* (London: Allen Lane, 2012)

Christopher Ryan & Cacilda Jetha, *Sex at Dawn: The Prehistoric Origins of Modern Sexuality* (New York: Harper Collins, 2010)

Cicely Veronica Wedgewood, *The Thirty Years War* (New York, The New York Review of Books, 2005)

Clive Trebilcock, *The Industrialization of the Continental Powers 1780 – 1914* (New York: Longman, 1992)

Dani Rodrik, *The Globalisation Paradox: Democracy and the Future of the World Economy* (New York: W.W. Norton & Company, 2011)

Dani Rodrik, *Economics Rules: The Rights and Wrongs of the Dismal Science* (New York: W.W. Norton & Company, 2015)

Daniel Kahneman, *Thinking Fast and Slow* (New York: Farrar, Straus and Giroux, 2011)

Danielle DiMartino Booth, *Fed Up: An Insider's Take on Why the Federal Reserve is Bad for America* (New York: Portfolio, 2017)

David Graeber, *Debt: The First 5000 Years* (Brooklyn, New York: Melville House, 2014)

David Graeber, *The Utopia of Rules: On Technology, Stupidity, and the Secret Joys of Bureaucracy* (Brooklyn, New York: Melville House, 2015)

David Harvey, *A Brief History of Neoliberalism* (New York: Oxford University Press, 2005)

David O. Sacks & Peter A. Thiel, *The Diversity Myth: Multiculturalism and Political Intolerance on Campus* (Oakland, CA: The Independent Institute, 1998)

Dean Baker, *Rigged: How Globalization and the Rules of the Modern Economy were Structured to Make the Rich Richer* (Washington, DC: Center for Economic and Policy Research, 2016)

Dinesh D'Souza, *The Big Lie: Exposing the Nazi Roots of the American Left* (Washington DC: Regnery Publishing, 2017)

Dinesh D'Souza, *What's So Great About Christianity* (Washington DC: Regnery Publishing, 2007)

Edward Griffin, *The Creature From Jekyll Island: A Second Look at the Federal Reserve* (Westlake Village, CA: American Media, 2010)

Elizabeth Economy, *By All Means Necessary: How China's Resource Quest is changing the World* (New York: Oxford University Press, 2014)

Elizabeth Popp Berman, *Creating the Market University: How Academic Science Became an Economic Engine* (Princeton, New Jersey: Princeton University Press, 2012)

Eugene Rogan, *The Fall of the Ottomans: The Great War in the Middle East* (New York: Basic Books, 2015)

Fred Block & Margaret R. Somers, *The Power of Market Fundamentalism: Karl Polanyi's Critique* (Cambridge, MA: Harvard University Press, 2014)

Frederik Obermaier & Bastian Obermayer, *The Panama Papers: Breaking the Story of How the Rich and Powerful Hide their Money* (London: Oneworld Publications, 2017)

Gabriel Zucman, *The Hidden Wealth of Nations: The Scourge of Tax Havens* (Chicago: The University of Chicago Press, 2015)

Gabriele Kuby, *The Global Sexual Revolution: Destruction of Freedom in the Name of Freedom* (Kettering, OH: Angelico Press, 2015)

Geoff Mortimer, *Eyewitness Accounts of the Thirty Years War 1618 – 48* (New York: Palgrave, 2002)

Gilbert Rist, *The Delusions of Economics: The Misguided Certainties of a Hazardous Science* (London: Zed Books, 2011)

Glenn Beck, *Liars: How Progressives Exploit Our Fears for Power and Control* (New York: Threshold Editions Subsidiary, 2016)

Gustave Le Bon, *The Crowd: A Study of the Popular Mind* (Mineola, New York: Dover Publications, 2002)

Guy Standing, *The Corruption of Capitalism: Why Rentiers Thrive and Work does not Pay* (London: Biteback Publishing Ltd, 2016)

Herbert I. Weisberg, *Willful Ignorance: The Mismeasure of Uncertainty* (Hoboken, New Jersey: John Wiley & Sons, 2014)

Hyman Minsky, *Stabilizing an Unstable Economy* (New York: McGraw-Hill Education, 2008)

J. Salwyn Schapiro, *Liberalism: Its Meaning and History* (Malabar, FL: Krieger, 1988)

Jacob S. Hacker & Paul Pierson, *American Amnesia: How the War on Government led us to Forget What Made America Prosper* (New York: Simon & Schuster, 2016)

Jacob S. Hacker & Paul Pierson, *Winner-Take-All Politics: How Washington Made the Rich Richer– And Turned Its Back on the Middle Class* (New York: Simon & Schuster, 2010)

James Burnham, *Suicide of the West: An Essay on the Meaning and Destiny of Liberalism* (New York: Encounter Books, 2014)

James K. Galbraith, *Inequality and Instability: A Study of the World Economy Just Before the Great Crisis* (New York: Oxford University Press, 2012)

James K. Galbraith, *The End of Normal: The Great Crisis and the Future of Growth* (New York: Simon & Schuster, 2014)

James Robinson, *Why Nations Fail: The Origins of Power, Prosperity, and Poverty* (New York: Crown Publishers, 2012)

Jan Luiten van Zanden, *The Long Road to the Industrial Revolution: The European Economy in a Global Perspective 1000 – 1800* (Leiden: Brill, 2009)

Jane Mayer, *Dark Money: The Hidden History of the Billionaires Behind the Rise of the Radical Right* (New York: Double Day, 2016)

Jean-Philippe Delsol, Nicholas Lecaussin, & Emmanuel Martin, *Anti-Piketty: Capital for the 21st-Century* (Washington DC: Cato Institute, 2017)

Jennifer Bachner & Benjamin Ginsberg, *What Washington Gets Wrong: The Unelected Officials Who Actually Run the Government and Their Misconceptions about the American People* (Amherst, New York: Prometheus Books, 2016)

Joe Earle, Cahal Moran & Zach Ward-Perkins, *The Econocracy: The Perils of Leaving Economics to the Experts* (Manchester: Manchester University Press, 2017)

John Brooks, *Once in Golconda: A True Drama of Wall Street 1920 – 1938* (New York: Open Road Integrated Media, 2014)

John Kay, *Other People's Money: Masters of the Universe or Servants of the People* (London: Profile Books, 2015)

John Maynard Keynes, *Essays in Persuasion* (New York: W.W. Norton & Company, 1963)

John Maynard Keynes, *The Economic Consequences of the Peace* (New York: Harcourt, Brace and Howe, 1920)

Jonah Goldberg, *Liberal Fascism: The Secret History of the American Left from Mussolini to the Politics of Meaning* (New York: Double Day, 2007)

Jonathan Haidt, *The Righteous Mind: Why Good People are Divided by Politics and Religion* (New York: Pantheon Books, 2012)

Joseph Heath, *Economics Without Illusions: Debunking the Myths of Modern Capitalism* (New York: Broadway Books, 2010)

Joseph S. Nye, Jr., *Is the American Century Over?* (Malden, MA: Polity Press, 2015)

Joseph Stiglitz, *Globalization and its Discontents* (New York: The Penguin Group, 2002)

Karl Polanyi, *The Great Transformation* (Boston, MA: Beacon Press, 2001)

Keith Lowe, *Savage Continent: Europe in the Aftermath of World War II* (New York: St. Martin's Press, 2012)

Kim R. Holmes, *The Closing of the Liberal Mind: How Groupthink and Intolerance Define the Left* (New York: Encounter Books, 2016)

Kirsten Powers, *The Silencing: How the Left is Killing Free Speech* (Washington DC: Regnery Publishing, 2015)

Laura Ingraham, *Shut Up & Sing: How Elites from Hollywood, Politics, and the Media Are Subverting America* (Washington DC: Regnery Publishing, 2003)

Laurence Rees, *Hitler's Charisma: Leading Millions into the Abyss* (New York: Pantheon Books, 2012)

Laurence Rees, *Horros in the East: Japan and the Atrocities of World War II* (London: Perseus Books Group, 2001)

Leif Wenar, *Blood Oil: Tyrants, Violence and the Rules that Run the World* (New York: Oxford University Press, 2016)

Liaquat Ahamed, *Lords of Finance: The Bankers Who Broke the World* (New York: The Penguin Press, 2009)

Mariana Mazzucato, *The Entrepreneurial State: Debunking Public vs. Private Sector Myths* (London: Anthem Press, 2013)

Mark Blyth, *Austerity: The History of a Dangerous Idea* (New York: Oxford University Press, 2013)

Mark Blyth, *Great Transformation: Economic Ideas and Institutional Change in the Twentieth Century* (New York: Cambridge University Press, 2002)

Mark Levin, *Men in Black: How the Supreme Court is Destroying America* (Washington DC: Regnery Publishing, 2005)

Mark Levin, *Plunder and Deceit: Big Government's Exploitation of Young People and the Future* (New York: Threshold Editions, 2015)

Mark Levin, *Rediscovering Americanism: And the Tyranny of Progressivism* (New York: Threshold Editions, 2017)

Martin Ford, *The Rise of Robots: Technology and the Threat of a Jobless Future* (New York: Basic Books, 2015)

Martyn Whittock, *The Third Reich: The Rise and fall of the Nazis* (London: Constable & Robinson Ltd, 2011)

Mervyn King, *The End of Alchemy: Money, Banking, and the Future of the Global Economy* (New York: W.W. Norton & Company, 2016)

Michael Dobbs, *One Minute to Midnight: Kennedy, Khrushchev, and Castro on the Brink of Nuclear War* (New York: Alfred Knopf, 2008)

Michael Kennedy, *The Jacobin Clubs in the French Revolution, 1793 – 1795* (New York: Berghahn Books, 2000)

Michael Walsh, *The Devil's Pleasure Palace: The Cult of Critical Theory and the Subversion of the West* (New York: Encounter Books, 2015)

Nassim Nicholas Taleb, *Skin in the Game: Hidden Asymmetries in Daily Life* (New York: Random House, 2018)

Neil Irwin, *The Alchemists: Three Central Bankers and A World on Fire* (New York: The Penguin Press, 2013)

Neil MacGregor, *Germany: Memories of a Nation* (London: Allen Lane, 2014)

Niall Ferguson, *Colossus: The Rise and fall of the American Empire* (New York: Penguin Books Ltd, 2005)

Niall Ferguson, *The Pity of War: Explaining World War I* (London: Allen Lane, 1998)

Nicholas Wapshott, *Keynes Hayek: The Clash that Defined Modern Economics* (New York: W.W. Norton & Company, 2011)

Peter H. Wilson, *The Thirty Years War: Europe's Tragedy* (Cambridge, MA: Harvard University Press, 2009)

Peter Schweizer, *Extortion: How Politicians Extract Your Money, Buy Votes, and Line Their Own Pockets* (New York: Houghton Mifflin Harcourt Publishing Company, 2013)

Philip Augar, *The Greed Merchants: How the Investment Banks Played the Free Market Game* (New York: Penguin Group, 2005)

Phillip Vincent, *The Lamentations of Germany* (London: Iohn Rothwell, 1638) available at Yale University Library <https://brbl-dl.library.yale.edu/vufind/Record/3445506>

Richard A. Posner, *The Crisis of Capitalist Democracy* (Cambridge, MA: Harvard University Press, 2010)

Robert Gordon, *The Rise and fall of American Growth: The US Standard of Living Since the Civil War* (Princeton, New Jersey: Princeton University Press, 2016)

Robert Gerwarth, *The Vanquished: Why the First World War Failed to End* (New York: Farrar, Straus and Giroux, 2016)

Robert Shaw, *The Epidemic: The Rot of American Culture, Absentee and Permissive Parenting, and the Resultant Plague of Joyless, Selfish Children* (New York: Harper Collins, 2003)

Robert Shiller, *Irrational Exuberance* (Princeton, New Jersey: Princeton University Press, 2015)

Robert Skidelsky, *Keynes: The Return of the Master* (New York: Public Affairs, 2010)

Robert Tombs, *The English and Their History* (New York: Alfred Knopf, 2014)

Roger Scruton, *On Human Nature* (Princeton, New Jersey: Princeton University Press, 2017)

Ryszard Legutko, *The Demon in Democracy: Totalitarian Temptations in Free Societies* (New York: Encounter Books, 2016)

Scott Greer, *No Campus for White Men: The Transformation of Higher Education into Hateful Indoctrination* (Washington DC: WND Books, 2017)

Sharyl Attkisson, *Stonewalled: My Fight for Truth Against the Forces of Obstruction, Intimidation, and Harassment in Obama's Washington* (New York: Harper Collins, 2014)

Sharyl Attkisson, *The Smear: How Shady Political Operatives and Fake News Control What You See, What You Think, and How You Vote* (New York: Harper Collins, 2017)

Shivaji Lokam, *The General Theory of Rapid Economic Development* (Hyderabad: Entropy Works, 2018)

Stephen Kotklin, *Armageddon Averted: The Soviet Collapse 1970 – 2000* (New York: Oxford University Press, 2008)

Steve Keen, *Debunking Economics: Naked Emperor Dethroned* (London: Zed Books, 2011)

Thomas Pikkety, *Capital in the Twenty-First Century* (Cambridge, MA: Harvard University Press, 2014)

Thorstein Veblen, *Imperial Germany and The Industrial Revolution* (Kitchener: Batoche Books, 2003)

Tom Burgis, *The Looting Machine: Warlords, Tycoons, Smugglers and the Systematic Theft of Africa's Wealth* (London: Harper Collins, 2015)

Tom Fitton, *Clean House: Exposing Our Government's Secrets and Lies* (New York: Simon & Schuster, 2016)

Tony Judt, *Ill Fares the Land* (New York: The Penguin Press, 2010)

Tony Judt, *Postwar: A History of Europe Since 1945* (New York: Penguin Books Ltd, 2005)

Vaclav Smil, *Creating the Twentieth Century: Technical Innovations of 1867 – 1914* (New York: Oxford University Press, 2013)

Vaclav Smil, *Made in the USA: The Rise and Retreat of American Manufacturing* (Cambridge, MA: The MIT Press, 2013)

Vaclav Smil, *Why America is Not a New Rome* (Cambridge, MA: The MIT Press, 2010)

Will Durant & Ariel Durant, *Rousseau and Revolution: The Story of Civilization* (New York: Simon & Schuster, 1967)

Will Durant, *Our Oriental Heritage: The Story of Civilization* (New York: Simon & Schuster, 1935)

William J. Murray, *Enslaving America and the World with Central Planning* (Washington DC: WND Books, 2016)

Index

A

Affordable Care Act, 187
Age of Colonial Expansion, 33,
    55, 89, 91, 139, 140
Age of Consolidation of
    Liberalism, 33, 161, 177, 182,
    184, 188
    Backstory, 115–19
Age of Discovery, 51
Age of Exploration, 52
Age of Industrial Revolution, 32,
    58, 94, 128, 171, 183, 241,
    246
Age of Mass Politics, 103
Age of Modernization, 32, 33, 60,
    64, 94, 110, 112, 115, 116,
    117, 118, 119, 171, 222, 244,
    246
Age of Nation-state, 31, 32, 56,
    84, 115
    Definition of Nation-state, 56
    Three Waves of Formation, 56
Age of Post-Darwin, 33, 64, 110,
    112, 118, 197
Age of Pre-Darwin, 32, 64
Age of Pre-Industry, 32, 57, 202
Age of Rise of Liberalism, 33
Age of Speculation, Expansion,
    Inversion, and Late Electronics
    Industry, 32, 62
Age of Supranational Polity, 32,
    57, 110, 115, 118, 119
Alexandra, Empress, 10
Alsace and Lorraine, 84
American founding fathers, 21,
    22, 24, 112, 182, 184, 193
Anarchy
    About, 140–42

Ancién Regime, 95, 145
Antifa, 187
Armageddon, 245
Arrow, Kenneth & Debreu,
    Gerard, 203

B

Baby Boomers, 188
Bacon, Francis, 12, 14
Banks
    How Money is Created, 236
    Role, 205
Bastille, 194
Beveridge Report, 107
Bill of Rights
    American, 23, 188, 194
    English, 19
Bolsheviks, 9, 10
Bretton Woods, 233, 264
Brexit, 184
British Empire, 53, 183
Burnham, James, 113, 114, 244,
    267

C

Capital, 48–49
    Capital goods
        Definition, 41
    Classification, 40
    How to Distinguish, 43
Capitalism
    Balance Sheet & Income
        Statement Interlink, 210–
        12
    England, 21
    Functioning, 206–12
Censorship, 162, 163, 176, 185

Christianity, 26, 198, 246, 247, 255, 256, 265
Classification of Economic Activity
Based on Kind, 35
Based on Value Addition, 34
Cold War, 3, 10, 245
Colonization
Aggression, 89
Effects, 241
Emigration, 121
History, 51–55
Retreat, 113
Scramble for Africa, 52, 54, 81
Comintern, 101
Committee of Public Safety, 195
Common Core, 116
Communism, 3, 71, 98, 99, 113, 133, 134, 138, 140, 164, 196, 242
Relationship with Fascism, 134–40
Comte, Auguste, 95
Constantine I, Emperor, 256
Cult of Reason, 13, 198
Cultural Marxism, 102, 109
Culture
Anti-war Stance, 123–24
Assault on Traditions, 156
Dilution, 121
Indoctrination, 112, 116
National Anthem, 115
Traditional Marriage, 109, 137
Transformation, 110–12

D

Darwin, Charles, 17, 32, 33, 64, 96, 97, 99, 112
Darwinism, 247
Declaration of Independence, 20, 32, 112, 194
Democratic Centralism, 157
Democratic Socialism, 243
Descartes, Rene, 12, 14

Developing Economies, 249
Dewey, John, 152
Diversity, 122, 161, 265

E

East Germany, 221
Economic Development
Concept, 48
Education
Fallacy, 152
Impact after the 1970s, 155
Liberal elite, 146
State control of, 163
Electoral College, 23, 184, 188
Emergency Conditions, 104, 105, 134, 167, 243
Enlightenment, 18, 21, 22, 95, 96, 97, 145, 191, 193, 197, 201
American founding fathers, 21
Equal Rights, 123
Eugenics, 163
European Union, 32, 57, 183

F

Fascism, 3, 71, 88, 91, 98, 99, 100, 103, 131, 133, 134, 135, 136, 137, 139, 140, 163, 164, 165, 166, 181, 196, 242
Relationship with Modern Liberalism, 163–67
Federal Reserve, 105, 172, 237, 254, 264, 265
Federal Trade Commission, 105
Federalism, 23
Fictitious Commodities, 73, 74, 80, 204
Financial Crisis 2008, 172
Causes, 230–33
pre-Crisis Period, 225–30
Role of Banking System, 238
Financial Services Modernization Act, 251
France
Colonial Possessions, 54

Currency stabilization, 133
Gold Reserves, 133
Lead upto Great War, 81
Postwar Savings, 62
Savings Rate, 60
Seven Years War, 241
Free Speech, 16, 21, 134, 160,
161, 164, 173, 176, 177, 182,
187
Policing of speech, 160
Freedom of the press, 160
French Revolution, 3, 13, 20, 95,
124, 193, 194, 195, 196, 197,
198, 241, 269

G

Gallup Poll
On Religious Views, 64–68
General Munitions Board, 105
General Will, 100, 191, 193, 194,
195, 196, 197, 198
Germany
End of Modernization, 218
Failure to Exit Gold Standard,
132
Nazi Germany, 135
Snyopsis of War history, 85
Unification, 87
Glass-Steagall Act, 251
Global South, 249
Global Wealth Databook, 47, 254
Gramsci, Antonio, 101, 109, 135
Great Awakening, 95–98, 145,
148
Great Britain
As Deterrance, 253
Exiting Gold Standard, 129
Identity, 183
Postwar Reforms, 107
Seven Years War, 241
Unemployment in the 1920s,
130
Great Britian
Exiting Gold Standard, 132
Great British

Dealing with Germany, 140
Great Depression
Causes, 233–37
Condition, 130–33
Role of France, 133
Great Recession, 233
Great War, 3, 9, 33, 55, 56, 60,
71, 73, 82, 93, 101, 102, 103,
105, 106, 113, 129, 133, 241,
242, 244, 245, 265

H

Hayek, Fredrick Von, 130, 131,
132, 270
Heavy Industry, 34, 36, 38, 39,
40, 41, 42, 43, 44, 46, 47, 48,
49, 59, 60, 128, 148, 154,
203, 204, 248
History
Seeing history, 88, 136, 242
Writing history, 27, 140
Hitler, Adolf, 91, 102, 103, 135,
139, 140, 268
Holocaust, 91, 135, 136, 139
Holy Roman Empire, 85, 86
Housing bubble, 225–27
Human Capital, 146, 151, 152,
153, 154, 155
Human Rights, 111, 115, 123,
136
Humanism, 123
Hume, David, 19

I

Immigration
Open Borders, 121
Industrial Revolution, 39, 42, 146,
151, 218, 252
Contriution to Growth, 153
Products, 38, 59
Significance, 151
International Gold Standard
About, 75
Analysis, 128

Correction, 93
Deflationary Forces, 78
Effects, 80
Gold flowing to France, 133
Operating History, 76
Workings, 76
Italian Social Republic, 135

J

Japan, 9, 67, 88, 89, 90, 91, 129,
140, 248, 268
Jobs, Steve, 149
Judeo-Christian Values, 98, 247

K

Kant, Immanuel, 199
Keynes, John Maynard, 129, 130,
131, 132, 204, 219, 264, 268,
270, 271

L

Laissez-faire
Pareto optimal outcome, 201
Laissez-faire Economics, 18, 19,
24, 25, 72, 73, 74, 79, 93, 94,
116, 127, 128, 132, 171, 192,
246, 247
Barter Exchange, 210
Ditch of Laissez-faire, 93
Free Capital Movement after
1990, 117
Gross Errors, 201-4
Pareto optimal outcome, 203
Professional Failure, 214
Question of Reappearance,
117
Late Electronics Industry, 64,
118, 149, 153
Communication platform
monopoly, 118
Late Electronics Revolution, 42,
63, 64, 176, 222
Latin American Depression, 254

Lenin, 6, 10, 102, 137, 139, 196
liberal elite, 115, 119, 121, 122,
142, 145, 146, 147, 148, 150,
152, 153, 154, 175, 177, 184,
187, 197
About, 145-53
Liberalism
Classical Liberalism, 11, 17,
25, 26, 100, 106, 110, 117,
127, 166, 167, 181, 182,
193, 201, 213, 242, 244,
245, 246, 247
Dimensions, 14
Global Reach, 19, 25
Good Society, 13, 16, 192,
193, 196
History, 12-16
Human Nature, 13-14, 192
Modern Liberalism, 11, 17,
26, 96, 99, 100, 106, 107,
109, 110, 112, 123, 138,
141, 145, 155, 157, 161,
163, 164, 165, 166, 167,
168, 181, 187, 244, 245,
246, 247, 256, 264, 268,
270
Relationship with reality, 27
Theoretical Development, 17-
18
Liberalization of Society
Discontents, 155-59
Process, 119-22
Locke, John, 18, 19, 20, 21, 182

M

Mandeville, Bernard, 201
Market Fundamentalism, 117
Marx, Karl, 79, 96, 97, 99, 100,
101, 102, 103, 137
Media, Academia and Arts
Language Engineering, 185-
87
Role, 163
Takeover, 115
Militarism, 140

Montesquieu, Charles, 22
Moore, Thomas, 96
Moroccan crises, 82
Mortgage Backed Securities, 223, 224, 225, 232
multiculturalism, 109, 121, 122, 156, 158
Munich Pact, 140
Mussolini, 91, 102, 135, 139, 163, 176, 181, 268

N

Napoleon, 52, 86, 243
Napoleonic Code, 243
NASDAQ, 64, 222, 223, 224
Nazism, 99, 133, 134, 136, 137, 140
Neoliberal order, 116
New World, 51, 52, 53, 247, 264
Nicholas II, 9
Nietzsche, Fredric, 17, 96, 98, 99, 102
NYSE, 223, 224

O

Old World, 55, 244
Orwell, George, 196

P

Paris Peace Conference, 82–84
Particle physics, 63, 222
political correctness, 160, 173
popular sovereignty, 24
Positivism, 12, 95
Private property, 72, 163, 165
Progressivism, 196
    Regressive nature, 162
    Rise in the US, 104–6
    Transformation to Modern Liberalism, 107
Propaganda
    Blame Game, 138
    Dissemination, 165

Media Tactics, 160
Postwar distortion of Events, 137
Public Infrastructure capital Limitations, 219

R

Reason
    Distinct Origins, 13
    Kant's Objection, 199
    Role, 13, 27, 95
Reformation, 85, 247, 256
Republicanism, 21, 22, 25, 107, 168, 171, 173, 182, 188, 191, 193, 194, 246
    Human Nature, 22
Ricardo, David, 19
Right to Bear Arms, 173, 182
    State control, 164
Rights of Man and of the Citizen, 194
Robespierre, Maximilian, 195
Roman Empire, 85, 254
Roosevelt, Franklin, 105, 106
Roosevelt, Theodore, 105
Rousseau, 19, 20, 197, 198, 272
Rousseau, Jean-Jacques, 12
Royal Navy, 253
Russian Empire, 9, 52, 71, 86

S

Say, Jean-Baptiste, 210
Say's Law, 210
Schumpeter, Joseph, 204
Scientific revolution, 14, 246
Second World War, 3, 6, 33, 55, 56, 60, 62, 71, 88, 91, 93, 106, 111, 113, 115, 119, 133, 136, 137, 138, 139, 140, 166, 244, 245, 253
Self-regulating market, 19, 72, 73, 74, 75, 76, 79, 80, 81, 88, 103, 106, 127, 128, 130, 131, 132, 181, 201, 213

September Massacres, 195
Seven Years War, 241, 242, 243
Smith, Adam, 19, 72, 201, 202,
    203, 204, 205, 206, 207, 210,
    212, 234, 236
social engineer, 146
Socialism, 3, 10, 99, 100, 103,
    129, 130, 134, 136, 137, 138,
    139, 196, 204, 242, 243, 247
Sorel, George, 101, 102, 135, 139
Soviet Union, 72, 245, 253
Speculative Investments, 62
St. Petersburg, 196
Statism, 97, 106, 242
Stock Market Crash, 1929, 106
Surveillance, 176

T

Taleb, Nassim Nicholas, 147,
    148, 154, 270
Textbook Democracy, 23, 184,
    188, 192
Theodosius I, Emperor, 256
Thirty-years War, 85–86
Totalitarianism, 131, 132, 196
Treaty of Versailles, 83, 84, 87
Triple Alliance, 81, 82
Triple Entente, 82

U

Uncertainty, 204
United Nations, 38, 57
United States
    Amendments to the
        Constitution, 172
    Constitution, 171
    Departure from Constitution,
        175
    Electoral College, 184
    Federalism, 173
    Founding Fathers, 161
    Gold in the early 1930s, 133
    In the 1920s, 133
    Narrative-making, 187
    Presidential Powers, 173
US Constitution, 22–25
Utopia, 193, 196, 213

V

Violence, 124, 139
Voltaire, 16, 97

W

Wall Street, 63, 222, 267
Western Power
    Conclusive Analysis, 244
    Decline in non-Western
        domain, 113
    Decline in Western Domain,
        119–22
    Enroachment of Enemy, 159–
        68
Wilson, Woodrow, 82, 83, 84,
    104, 105, 106, 146, 147, 172,
    270
World Peace, 123, 160, 253